Islam: A Religion, A Culture, A Society

Bill Schwartz

First published by Christians Aware 2014
Second Edition 2015

ISBN 978 1 873372 51 7

Printed by Creeds Telephone: **01308 423411** Web: **www.creedsuk.com**

Table of Contents

FOREWORD

I came to the Middle East as a student in the autumn of 1972 thinking it would be fun to do a "term abroad" with a group of like-minded friends. I had little doubt that it would be an interesting time. It was supposed to be an 'experience of learning' simply to enhance my overall education. Little did I know…

What started as a student "term-abroad" quickly became a life-changing experience. In the summer of 1973 I jumped at a job offer to return to Egypt to manage the programme (which extended to 1977). Not too long after settling into the term with a group of students the 1973 Arab-Israeli war began. We learned about blackouts and potential bombing raids. I also learned that many Egyptians deeply resented American political, economic and military support for the Israeli army, and that people in other countries view US foreign policy differently than what I had known, and presumed to be "right". The disconnected solidarity among the Arab countries that came about during that conflict, and the oil embargo, was confusing. It was about Islam, and it was about Arab brotherhood, but I couldn't work out how that had anything to do with the borders between Israel and Egypt, Syria and Jordan. I had a lot to learn.

My time in Egypt taught me that all life in the Middle East is inextricably influenced by Islam. I studied Islam as a religion, and I experienced it as a culture. From the beginning of my experience of the Middle East it was easy to see that my inherited American value of the separation of religion and politics did not even remotely apply. Eastern Christianity also became a fascination, particularly the long history of shared culture between Arab Christians and Muslims, and how that sharing has developed theological perspectives very differently from how Christian theology developed in the West. It was the beginning of understanding of Christianity as a minority ethnicity as well as the Dhimmi[1] classification. Very importantly I learned that not all Arabs are Muslims and not all Muslims are Arabs. (Later in life I also strongly affirm that not all Muslims are terrorists, and not all terrorists are Muslims!)

---

1 For a definition please see the Glossary.

Separately, but also important, during those five years in Egypt, Edith and I started our marriage and partnership in ministry. At our wedding she arranged for a friend to sing a song based on Ruth's words to Naomi, *"whither thou goest, I will go; and where thou lodgest, I will lodge"*. We both agree that she hasn't withered, but she certainly has been "going" ever since! We moved to Cyprus in 1977 and, with one thing leading to another, we lived there for 22 years. Cyprus was, and still is, a nexus for the Arab Christian world. During those years I had reason to visit almost every country of the Middle East many times, interacting with church and mission leaders of all backgrounds; Arab, European, Asian and African, and learning of their varied approaches to interaction with Muslims. Many were strongly motivated to convert Muslims to Christianity; on the other end of the spectrum, others were motivated simply to co-exist by trying to avoid interaction as much as possible. The single most obvious impression I took away from those years of experience was that Christians generally lack any interest to understand Muslims the way Muslims understand themselves.

During the eight years we lived in Saudi Arabia I found an abundant availability of "How to be a good Muslim" books in English, distributed for the benefit of Muslims who are not literate in Arabic. Obviously, these publications are aimed at Muslims who are intentional about their Islamic identity, but it would be a mistake to presume this literature is about fundamentalism; they closely resemble much of what is available in popular Christian bookstores in Europe and America. This literature provided much better insight into Islamic thinking and lifestyle than any Christian book about Islam that I have ever read. The opportunity to observe and experience a very fundamentalist cultural expression of Islam during those years also helped establish an awareness of the difference between fanaticism and piety among Muslims I interacted with on a daily basis.

Living and working in the countries of the Arabian peninsula for many years has shown me that the Arab world is not even remotely monolithic. Arab identity is very different in Iraq than in Egypt, in Kuwait than in Libya, in Palestine than in Yemen. Local customs and fatwas define daily life in Islam differently in different countries. Certainly the petrochemical wealth that emerged in the wake of the 1973 oil embargo changed these countries irrevocably, but it is impossible to evaluate which changes are "good" and which are "bad"; in each locality the local debate continues. Nevertheless, the resultant funding of a resurgent Islamic identity has changed the way Muslims are perceived throughout the world, for better or worse. Far too often that perception is driven by fear-mongering media hype and political expediency. Far too many people are willing to form opinions without substance and understanding. I sincerely hope this book contributes to both substance and understanding.

Appreciations are in order. I have had the privilege of not only reading books written by scholars on Islam and the Middle East, but also of deep personal friendships with many. Numerous dinner conversations over the years with Ken Bailey, Colin Chapman, Wendell Evans, Lew Scudder, Kenneth Cragg, and other authors helped me learn more deeply the insight in their writings. Spiritual guidance and theological perspective observed in the lives of many Middle Eastern Church leaders, both Western and Eastern, has deeply informed my understanding of the rich cultural and religious heritage of Islam, while at the same time strengthening my fundamental convictions around the Incarnational and Trinitarian revelation of God as received in Christian tradition. I must thank Dr David Grafton for his valuable guidance and support in the writing of this text. Without reservation I must thank my wife Edith for her encouragement to keep writing and ensuring I could have uninterrupted time at my computer – no easy task. Lastly, I must thank countless friends who, in conversations over many years, have struggled to understand their cultural disconnect while living in the Middle East. Searching for answers together formed the incentive and the end result which became this book. I can affirm wholeheartedly that the struggle is worthwhile and that those who do will not only understand Muslims better, but themselves as well.

INTRODUCTION

Since the event often referred to as "9/11", non-Muslims all around the world have become more motivated to try and understand Islam. There is now an increasing inventory of important and helpful literature comparing Islam and Christianity as religions, and some that focus on the clash of civilisations, or cultures. At the same time, there is a large and influential body of literature, news networks, and stereotyping in cinema and other mainstream media that significantly misrepresents (or at least distorts specificities of) Islam, and inevitably supports an alarmist perspective. In fact, most of this media attention does not really help Christians understand Islam, and very often broadens the gap between Christians and Muslims who are actually interested in dialogue and understanding. There is a need for a different approach toward achieving mutual understanding.[2]

Over a longer period of time, say the past forty years, the religious atmosphere all around the world has more and more noticeably polarised into conservative/liberal, or traditionalist/fundamentalist influences. This is especially true in the United States.[3] Certainly within both Islam and Christianity, there are growing popular movements which value a return to the basics, and a desire to recover a past period of *pure* religion.[4] For Christians, this often means a focus on *Biblical* practices (quite often from the Old Testament) in the Church, often accompanied by a rejection of denominational traditions and values.[5] For Muslims, it means a rejection of non-Islamic cultural accretions *(bid'a)*, the rise of secularism, and a desire to see the literal application of the *Sunnah*[6] more and more rigorously in society. In any attempt to understand fundamentalist trends in Islam it is

---

2 Appendix 1 presents a contrasting list of media to illustrate this point.

3 Barry A Cosmin and Juhem Nararro-Rivera, "The Transformation of Generation X: Shifts in Religious and Political Self-Identification, 1990-2008. A Report Based on the American Religious Identification Survey 2008", *Program on Public Values* (2012): 4-5

4 Karen Armstrong, The Battle for God, 1st ed. (New York: Alfred A. Knopf, 2000), 254, 266

5 Witness the rise in popularity of "bible churches", para-church organisations and non-denominational mega-churches in urban areas all over the USA.

6 The body of Islamic rulings which govern the way Muslims live. For clarity, Islamic terms and Arabic vocabulary are included for reference. Please refer to the Glossary at the end for Islamic definitions.

important to recognise similar trends in our own culture, and understand the difference between theological and cultural influences in both cultures in the analysis.

Living and working within a Arab Islamic cultural context, and observing the interplay of cultural[7] and religious values expressed in this polarisation during the last three decades, I have found that most literature written by Christians about Islam and literature written by Muslims about Christianity has been either polemic or apologetic in nature; usually written as a resource for a readership primarily interested in proselytising. Usually, comparisons are focused on something identified with 'good' in one culture and contrasted with something 'bad' in the other. Of course, any presentation of one religion through the filter of values and theology of another will very often misrepresent the 'other'. It follows that any movement toward honest interreligious dialogue is seriously hampered by these misrepresentations, while popular uninformed opinion becomes even more misinformed, polarised and antagonistic.

Since "9/11" many scholarly works have been written by both Muslims and Christians who have attempted to present a framework in which thinking Christians could possibly better understand Islam.[8] Some are specifically written for that purpose, while other scholarly writings are useful for understanding Islamic history, culture, politics and economics in an academic setting. Unfortunately, a full understanding of this literature is dependent upon a level of familiarity with Islam that is beyond the experience of most Western Christians. At the same time, in the West, and especially in America, most people encounter Islam through media coverage and foreign policy statements on the subject of terrorism and

---

7 For the purposes of this book I use the word 'culture' to refer to the attitudes and behaviour characteristics, usually unconsciously perceived and unconsciously expressed, of a particular social group. Of course these perceptions are usually generalised and often stereotyped, which is one of the motivating factors behind this particular study. "Culture is 'the more or less integrated systems of beliefs, feelings and values, and their associated symbols, patterns of behaviour and products shared by a group of people.'" Paul G Hiebert, "Cultural Differences and the Communication of the Gospel (Perspectives On the World Christian Movement)", *Wm Carey Library Press* (1981): 375.

8 It is noteworthy that it is not easy to find material written by Muslims with a view to helping other Muslims better understand Christianity.

unrest, rather than encountering Islam as a religious tradition and culture. Also, this unfortunately means that polemic, and polarising presentation, is what most Christians find familiar, accessible, and understandable in their attempts to define Islam.

Living in the Middle East over the past four decades and pastoring congregations in the Arab Peninsula for more than fourteen years has presented abundant opportunity to work with both Christians and Muslims who have inherited inaccurate presuppositions about each other's cultures and religions. People from all over the world come to the Middle East in a variety of professional capacities and find that the values and cultures there are very different from their home society. Not only do they find the adjustment difficult, but they also experience personal difficulty in explaining their life in the Middle East to friends and family back home. Life in the Middle East is just so very different.

Cultural values are generally subconscious until an event or circumstance brings them to the fore and challenges the way we think or the reasons behind our behavioural habits. In the Arabian Gulf it is customary to attend church on Friday, since that is the day of the week most people can be away from work. Sunday is a working day. Is Sunday worship an essential manifestation of our faith, or is it a cultural tradition of Christianity? Does one's Western understanding of the marriage relationship provide scope for understanding how multiple wives share the household chores and child-rearing responsibilities in a Muslim household? Most people don't bother to consider the relationship between their religious values and their cultural assumptions, and the socio/religious/cultural interchange between Muslims and Christians often highlight how much we incorrectly assume about each other.

The popular/traditional stereotypes, presuppositions and comparisons don't work very well. Non-Arab Christians living in Arab Muslim cultures inevitably find that Muslims are different from what they expected, based on what they have read and seen in public media, Christian books, and even in Bible study. Traditional comparisons of the Qur'an and the Bible, Muhammad and Jesus, Lent and Ramadan, etc., are actually very inaccurate and they inevitably reinforce Islamic misunderstandings of Christianity. To reach any level of success, serious dialogue, and especially meaningful evangelism, one must dispense with these incorrect associations.

Citing a prominent theme, I can say that many Christians who come to live in the Middle East find that an eschatological framework that idealises the current state of Israel as part of God's ultimate biblical plan is insupportable in the face of real life in this part of the world and especially real life in the Holy Land itself.[9] They also find that: very few Muslims support violence; not all Arabs are Muslims; many Muslims think Christians worship three gods; many Muslims think that Christians are predisposed to immorality – and much more. They also find the piety of Muslims who are even casual about their faith inspiring, while inconsistencies between piety and daily life are baffling. In the Middle East, religion permeates EVERYTHING – and truth, integrity and responsibility seem to have different cultural definitions. This disorientation leads to a steady stream of pastoral interactions as members of our congregations have struggled both to understand Islam and to adjust to life in Islamic societies.

This book is an attempt to help Christians understand Islam and Arab Islamic[10] cultural values from an Islamic point of view on a level that is accessible to 'average' church-going people. Because contrast and comparison are helpful tools for understanding, one facet of this book will attempt to identify *appropriate comparisons and contrasts* while presenting underlying concepts that define the way Arab Muslim and Western Christian religious understandings have produced very different cultural values and habits. It is my hope that, in presenting *appropriate* comparisons and contrasts, that any Muslim reading this text would find this book helpful for understanding Christianity and Christian cultural values. Mostly, it is my sincere hope that this text will enable Christians who interact with Muslims socially or commercially, better to comprehend Islamic values

---

9 The popularity of *Christian Zionism* (eschatologically based support for the political state of Israel) among Evangelicals, Pentecostals and even among some mainline Christians has confused many Muslims about what they see as the political nature of Christianity. For an in-depth presentation and a thorough survey of the history and theology of the problem see Colin Chapman's *Whose Promised Land*, Lion Paperback, 1992.

10 It is important to clarify that the majority of Muslims are not Arabs. In this study I will concentrate on Arab Islam, as the historical foundational roots of Islam and the standard upon which current Islamic radical "return to the roots' movements are referenced.

Construction/modernisation in Dubai, United Arab Emirates

and Islamic society. I also hope to enable Christians to present Christianity and the secular values that have become identified with Christian culture, which conservative Muslims consistently misinterpret, with more informed and accurate comparisons and explanations. And finally, I hope this text will contribute to more informed dialogue, simple interaction and, more importantly, a better witness of Christian identity and belief to all.

While living for more than a fifteen years in two different very traditionalist Islamic societies that are struggling with identity in the face of rapid modernisation, I have read and have attempted to understand a broad selection of Islamic publications written by Muslims for Muslims, written with the intent of encouraging purity in Islam and a resurgence of Islamic identity. I have interacted with Muslims from many different Islamic societies who have shared this experience of living the paradox of retaining a pure Islamic identity in the face of changes in the culture brought by very rapid modernisation.[11]

11 Judith Miller, *God Has Ninety-Nine Names: Reporting from a Militant Middle East* (New York: Simon & Schuster, 1996), 466-477

Construction/modernisation in Doha, Qatar

As an example, I have learned that the consistent characterisation by the media of a person or a society becoming "Westernised" is a grave insult to many Muslims. Muslims of the Middle East have no intention or desire to leave their Islamic identity in the past while embracing technology and other modernising influences, characterised by some Islamic conservatives as 'cultural invasion'. Many indeed are wary of any influence in their society that would corrupt their historic values and traditions. I would even state that this particular paradox is one of the driving forces toward Islamic radicalisation in current times. This book could be characterised as an attempt to distil those writings, and my experience over the past decades, in a presentation of Islam that would both satisfy Islamic self-perception and give Christians a framework for understanding, interaction and shared living with Muslims whether in the Middle East or in the West.

As a point of clarification, I should state that this book assumes that the reader doesn't need the traditional very basic introduction to Islam. Furthermore, this book is an attempt to focus on understanding the presentation of Islam and Islamic values in the way Islamic "purists" are attempting to define Islam.[12] Of course it is impossible to examine all of the facets of Islam in one book. It is important to understand that this "purist" presentation of Islam purports to represent Islam to all Muslims *and* to the rest of the world, in much the same way that post-denominational and "Evangelical" Christianity often purports to represent true Christianity, often denying the validity of any other Christian expression or tradition.[13] There are indeed reasons to disregard a radicalised or purist perspective, but there can be no denial that these influences are affecting mainline Christianity and Islam in all forms in all parts of the world. Therefore, these influences deserve our attention and, hopefully, our understanding.

Culture and religion are intertwined, but we experience these two forces of dynamism in life differently. For example, in the West we all know about

---

12 Islam, like Christianity, is experiencing a revivalist trend. There are conservative Muslims who would deny the validity of any Islamic expression other than their particular interpretation. Mainline co-religionists are not committed enough; our faith needs to be rescued from modernisation; leaders of government have 'sold out' to secular values; are all sentiments held in common between both Christian and Islamic fundamentalist movements seeking to regain a purity of religion as a solution to the problems of the world.

13 More and more commonly, conservative Christians are labeling mainline, liberal theological perspectives as 'unbiblical' or 'apostate', advocating separation as necessary to maintaining the purity of Christian faith. We have seen this polarisation in different waves during controversies over creationism, women in ordination, women in the episcopate, ordination of homosexuals, and in general, the literal interpretation of biblical texts.

the 'Christmas spirit' and Christians are very aware that secular and market influences have hijacked the religious heritage of God's love and peace expressed in the Christmas story. Similarly, in Islam, Ramadan is a month of fasting, mandated in the *Sunnah* and is a culturally unifying tradition in Islamic countries. Ramadan has also become commercialised in many places. Because Muslims must fast during the day and are allowed to eat and drink at night, restaurants and shop hours are often curtailed during the day while running promotions for all-night sales and special events. In many Arab countries food sales increase dramatically during Ramadan. Discerning how commercial influences have changed religious celebrations is one way of understanding the difference between cultural and religious influences is everyday life.

To this end, the chapters of this book will investigate concepts that are in some way shared by Western Christian culture and Arab Islamic culture, but at the same time generate very differing sets of values and understandings of life. For instance, Islam and Christianity share the reverence for prophets and scriptures, but the two religions have very different understandings of how, what and *why* God reveals. We will look at this in the first chapter on **The Purpose of Revelation**, followed by an exploration of how Christianity and Islam distinctively understand the nature of revelation in chapter two, **In the Beginning**. Of course, the way we define/understand God's existence and purpose also determines substantial differences in the way religious systems understand their appropriate response to God and revelation. We will look into this subject in **The Perception of God** in the third chapter.

Christianity and Islam perceive God differently, and therefore perceive humanity's responsibility to obey and follow God's revelation in very different ways. Christians know it is important to participate in the work of the Gospel, and Muslims are commanded to strive for the expansion of Islam. The fourth chapter on **Jihad and Ijtihad** will discuss the personal and corporate nature of the Muslim requirement to obey God's revelation and the Prophet Muhammad. The fifth and sixth chapters will deal with **Personal and Public Identity** in society that shapes the basis for **Choices and Responsibility** in the way people interact with each other within their cultural/religious value systems. These chapters will reflect on the way

Islam as a religion is expressed in social relationships and cultural norms, with some comparison of how Secularism has had a very different effect on Western Christian identity. These chapters will also explore foundational cultural values that are shared by both Christians and Muslims, while at the same time being expressed very differently, like concepts of *right and wrong* and *honour and shame*. Hopefully, these insights will better inform a broad spectrum of encounter between Christians and Muslims in the workplace, in the supermarket, in traffic, in social conversation, in the frustration of having to cope with necessary changes in lifestyle, and especially in the conversations we have between us about how our religious traditions form our lives.

The seventh chapter analysing what is permitted and forbidden, **Clean and Unclean**, will review how many cultural customs have developed from this particular consciousness in Islam over the centuries. It will offer a perspective for contrasting Western Christianity's secular world-view, with increasing separation between religious and civil functions of society, and hopefully give insight regarding the increasing Islamic rejection of secular influences as inappropriate colonial impositions in Muslim countries. The eighth chapter, **Religion and Society**, will expand the discussion by specifically looking at the relationship between religious and secular values as perceived by Muslims.

The ninth chapter examines ways in which current developments regarding **Human Rights**, in varying expressions, are a constant source of conflict and misunderstanding between Christian/secular cultures and conservative Islamic values. However, the context for understanding issues relating to Human Rights must come within a framework that recognises the secular origins of the Human Rights movement, and also recognises that not all countries value secularism.

Muslims everywhere are anxious to discuss religious issues and share Islam with Christians they meet. Unfortunately most Christians, including clergy, are ill-prepared to interact with their Muslim friends in an informed, honest and confident dialogue. The tenth chapter, **Christian-Muslim Dialogue**, will attempt to provide some guidance for people who interact with Muslims in social *and* religious dialogue both formally and informally.

For Christians whose employment offers the experience of living within Islamic cultural contexts, these clarifications could enable people better to understand and enjoy that opportunity, and hopefully will help lead to better relationships. Finally, the **Conclusion** will offer a theological perspective on the Christian-Muslim encounter. It will highlight challenges and opportunities for Christians living in a Muslim culture in the Arabian Peninsula. Mostly, I hope the presentation of concepts in this way will provide a foundation for Christians to "always be ready to make your defence to anyone who demands from you an accounting for the hope that is in you." (*1 Peter 3:15*) I also hope that it will enable Christians living in Arab Islamic cultures to engage in relationships with Muslim friends and colleagues with understanding and openness, valuing and learning from these relationships and growing in their own Christian faith.

As something of a postscript I want to add that in the months after 9/11 I was often asked by American friends, "Why do they hate us?" To my amazement, even though the question was asked quite often and with real sincerity, very few of those who asked really showed any interest in pursuing discussion toward exploring that question. In fact, I found that it was considered unpatriotic to even consider that the question could be valid. I hope that this book can also offer the reader some insight; not about 'why they hate us' but rather that conservative Muslims perceive "us" completely different than the way we perceive ourselves. It should follow that Christians don't easily/readily perceive Islam as Muslims do, and that meaningful interaction, much less meaningful dialogue, is hindered by this difficulty. I sincerely hope this book bridges that gap in a helpful way.

1. THE PURPOSE OF REVELATION

How we perceive the nature of revelation is inextricably determined by how we perceive the purpose of revelation.

A central premise of this book is that Christians and Muslims continually miscomprehend each other's religious values because each typically encounters the "other" religion through the filter of their own religious presuppositions. To understand this problem, and hopefully address it in a helpful manner, the subtleties of the relationship between purpose and nature in God's revelation are tremendously significant. At the same time, we can perhaps better understand our own religious perceptions through contrasting how another religious system understands revelation.

The essential beliefs in Islam can only rightly comprehended within the Islamic concepts of *Tawheed*[14] and *Shirk*.[15]

> This is what Islam considers to be the fundamental error at the root of all sin or transgression. It is the "association" of something with God, other than God Himself. God is the Absolute. This means that he is Complete. He is Totality. He is Reality. Nothing can be added to Him, and nothing can be taken away. He is one and Indivisible.
>
> To set anything alongside God as Reality is to commit the sin – the error that engages our consciousness and our being – of "association", which is the only sin that God cannot forgive, because it denies Himself, and prevents forgiveness:
>
> *God forgives not that aught should be with Him associated; less than that He forgives to whomsoever he will. Whoso associates with God anything, has gone astray into far error.* (4:116).
>
> The sin of *shirk* ("association") is a name for paganism; pagans are called "the associators" (mushrikūn). But *shirk* is the fundamental state of being in revolt against God, irrespective of any professed belief in other gods. It is also atheism or the putting of nothingness in the place of God. *Shirk* is the opposite of surrender to God, which

14 The acknowledging of the Unity of God, the indivisible, Absolute, and the sole Real.

15 The "association" of something with God, other than God Himself.

is acceptance and recognition of His Reality: knowledge, or Islam. Because Islam is knowledge, it is initiated by the act of recognition: the *shahadah*. The *shahadah* is perceiving and declaring that "there is no god but God".[16]

In Islam *Allah*[17] is utterly "one" *and* utterly "other". Nothing created can be associated with God. Neither is God "in relationship" with anything created.[18] Consequently, humans cannot "know" God. When a Christian claims to have a personal relationship with God through Jesus Christ, a moderate Muslim would view the statement as presumptuous. A conservative Muslim would see it as blasphemous. At best, Islam proposes that human beings cannot comprehend God, but rather his *purpose for human society*.

It is also to be emphasised that "revelation" in the Islamic tradition is not incarnation; rather it is purely ideational. This is understandable in terms of the uncompromising Islamic attitude on the transcendence of God. However, owing to the relatively optimistic view of the human nature, there was no need that God's *being* be revealed for the sake of human salvation or redemption. What was revealed, therefore, was God's guidance or will, which is "wholly the ethically-imperative, the commandment, the law.[19]

Islam understands God's revelation, commonly known as the *Sunnah*, as a gift to humanity to show the "true path" for living correctly in this life, to the end that rewards in heaven can be obtained and punishments in hell can be avoided in the afterlife. As the eminent American Evangelical Islamicist, Dudley Woodbury, notes: "Since the *Qur'an* portrays the human

16 Cyril Glassé, *The New Encyclopedia of Islam, Rev. ed.* (Walnut Creek, CA: AltaMira Press, 2001): 428.

17 Literally, the Arabic word for "the God". It is essential to state at the very beginning that Arabic speaking people, Jewish, Christian and Muslim all use the same Arabic word in reference to God. This is discussed in much more detail in chapter 3.

18 Abdullah Yusuf Ali, *An English Interpretation of the Holy Qur-an with Full Arabic Text.* (Lahore: Sh. Mu-hammad Ashraf, 1975, 1976), 785. (commentary note 2529, on Surah 19, vv 88-89, states: "The belief in God begetting a son is not a question merely of words or of speculative thought. It is a stupendous blasphemy against God. It lowers God to the level of an animal. If combined with the doctrine of vicarious atonement, it amounts to a negation of God's justice and man's personal responsibility. It is destructive of all moral and spritual order, and is condemned in the strongest possible terms.")

19 Zafar I Ansari, "Some Reflections on Islamic Bases for Dialogue with Jews and Christians," *Journal of Ecumenical Studies* 14, no. 3 (June 1, 1977) 435. (italics mine)

predicament as primarily ignorance rather than evil, as in the biblical analysis, the Muslim sees only the need of a guide, not a saviour."[20] People are not reconciled to God, but guided in right social relationships. Obedience brings rewards in heaven/afterlife, but there is no sense of redemption in the event of disobedience to *Shari'a*.[21]

It should be obvious that these two understandings are not only incompatible, but antithetical. It also follows, therefore, that for the two different religions revelation itself has a different purpose. It is not my intention to elaborate on the fact that these differing concepts are mutually exclusive, but that they determine a very different sense of the appropriate response to revelation. To reiterate, the purpose of revelation as Christianity understands it is that God is revealing his *self* (nature), with the intention of relationship, while in the Islamic understanding of revelation God is revealing the "true path" for humanity with the intention of teaching humanity how to live. To say this in another way, Islam does not – cannot – perceive God as revealing *himself*, which is the very essential understanding of the purpose of revelation in Christianity.

Inherent in the essential Christian doctrine of the Incarnation is the conviction that in Jesus the nature of God is revealed and that something of "Godness" indwells creation. Furthermore, Christians understand that God's intervention/participation in creation *in human form* redeems the creation, and particularly human nature, from corruption and separation from God – to the end that God has imparted something of himself into redeemed humanity.[22] Christians call this threefold experience of God "Trinity". While that may seem elementary to some, it presumes a number of things; among them that God wants to be known, that he is knowable, that humans can participate in this knowledge in some way, that there is a divine connection between God and creation most visibly comprehended in the connection between God and humanity, particularly in the humanity of Jesus Christ. This understanding of God most emphatically presumes

---

20 J Dudley Woodberry, "The Muslim Understanding of Jesus," *Word & World* 16, no. 2 (March 1, 1996): 177.

21 Islamic canonical law based on the teachings of the Koran and the traditions of the Prophet.

22 Christians understand this concept as the gift of the Holy Spirit most notably recorded in Acts 2.

that God is engaged in an ongoing relationship with his creation and his creatures. However, this idea of a dynamic relationship between God and creation is repudiated in Islam. In Islam God cannot be understood or experienced because God is utterly transcendental. In Islam revelation is not about God; but about laws he has presented for guidance of society and the welfare of humanity. We will return to this concept in the conclusion.

Christians understand the purpose of revelation as an invitation to be reconciled with God. This reconciliation is available to creation through the life and saving acts of Jesus who is the unity of God and humanity in one being. Therefore revelation is dynamic, ongoing; past, present and future – in spite of the fact that the person of Jesus is rooted in time, place and culture. In Christianity revelation is understood to transcend time, language, culture and ethnicity. Revelation in Islam is not, and cannot be, relational, but is expressed in written text known as the *Qur'an*. Coupled with, though not on the same 'level' as the *Qur'an*, are published collections of the "sayings" of Muhammad, collectively known as the *Hadith*. The juridical interpretation of *Qur'an* and *Hadith*[23] together are known in Islam as *The Sunnah*. As such, it is static; defined and rooted in time and place and language, and to a significant degree within the specificity Muhammad's life, and Arab culture. The connection between the purpose and nature of revelation as perceived by the two different religions and respective cultures can only be understood in this contrast.

And here we need careful clarification. The Arabic word "Islam" means 'submission'. While it of course applies to individual submission to God's revelation, in Arab culture the individual's identity is derived from family, tribe and community. The *Qur'an*, and more importantly the *Hadith*, represent God's law and guidance for society, and the individual's relationship to society, not the individual's relationship to God himself. Because God is unknowable and utterly "other", the concept of being reconciled to God is foreign to orthodox Islam.[24]

Of course, both Christian and Islamic traditions emphasize that God's

---

23 The vast collection of traditions containing sayings of the prophet Muhammad.

24 The Sufi tradition in Islam does seek a personal intimate relationship with God, but the modern trend toward conservatism in Islam rejects this idea as syncretistic.

essential identity embodies power and authority, and his very essence demands submission. To develop this contrast in a different way, one can realise that it is possible for Christianity to be perceived in purely personal terms, while the corporate/communal nature of humanity's response to revelation is essential in Islam. To understand this contrast more fully it is useful to say that in Islam the individual relates to society, not to God. Obedience/submission to God's law (*Shari'a*) is the manifestation of submission to God. The Christian understanding of revelation is that God desires a loving relationship with his creatures and has revealed him*self*.

The differences here are subtle. Of course Christian teaching presumes community. The *ekklesia*[25] represents those whom God has called/chosen to form a community/body/family adopted into relationship with Him through the redemptive life, death, resurrection and ascension of Jesus. In Christianity, relationship with God cannot be properly expressed outside of relationship with fellow human beings, and all of creation for that matter. Conversely, the relationship with God that is mostly corporate/communal, without a personal interaction with God, is incomplete in the Christian understanding. One way of expressing the subtlety would be to say that a Christian relationship with God must *always* be personal but *never* individualistic. It must always reflect the Christian understanding of God's Trinitarian, relational nature, which desires reconciliation with all of creation.

Islam has no concept of original sin.[26] The Christian theological premise that human sin is the basis of a separation between God and man is not understood in Islam because in Islam the separation is found in the nature of God himself who is so totally "other". There is no possibility of personal relationship because humans cannot comprehend God. Anglican Islamicist, Colin Chapman, notes that in Islam,

> God's response to the weakness of humankind is to provide guidance (*hidaya*) that will show people how to follow 'the straight path' (*al-sirat al-mustaqim*); a model of how Muslims should live; and the Islamic community… The basic emphasis of Islamic salvation lies

---

25 The Greek word in the New Testament denoting 'assembly' and 'church'.

26 Glassé, 431.

> instead in the historical responsibility of its followers, namely the establishment of the ideal religio-political order with a worldwide membership of all those who believe in God and His revelation through Muhammad, upon whom be peace.[27]

Understanding how differently Christianity and Islam perceive the substance and purpose of revelation should provide some clarity about our differing values, but it also raises a number of additional questions. Subsequent chapters will investigate how this affects our different perceptions of God's intention for humanity and generates cultural norms that are often mutually misunderstood. We will move on to discussion about how our differing perceptions of God, his nature, his purpose and the flow of revelation influences mutual misunderstanding between Muslims and Christians.

27 Colin Chapman, *The Bible Through Muslim Eyes, and a Christian Response.* (Cambridge: Grove Books, 2008), 28.

2. IN THE BEGINNING

Christians who wish to understand Islam by its own definition must begin with a commitment to understanding how Islam perceives the nature of God, as well as the flow and the purpose of God's revelation.

Christians, in the historic and Biblical tradition, have received revelation of an immanent covenantal God whose presence permanently pervades and sustains the universe. It is a fundamental tenet of Christianity that God desires to be known. He created humanity to be in relationship with him as persons and as a society. God, in Christian tradition, knows the frailty of creation and personally intervenes to reconcile all of creation to himself (2Co 5:19). Christians understand this reconciling process as past, current and future most comprehensively revealed in God's act of entering/participating in creation by *becoming human* in Jesus Christ, and thereby redeeming creation by his presence through his redeeming participation in all that is created, in his birth, life, death, resurrection and ascension. Christians believe that we are brought into reconciled relationship with each other and with God through *God's initiative*, which we experience historically in Jesus Christ, and contemporarily in the imparting of God's Spirit in our daily lives. In common conversation Christians refer to this process as salvation.

Muslims perceive the purpose of revelation quite differently. Most importantly, Muslims understand God to be eternally transcendent, existing apart from, and cannot be subject to, the limitations of the material universe in any way.

> "The literal translation of '*fis-sama*' is 'in heavens', the scholars explained it according to the Arabic language to have the meaning of (above) as it is not possible for Allah to be surrounded by His creation…"[28]

In Islam, *Allah* gifted the *Qur'an*, his revelation of monotheism, to different Muslims of history. Islam teaches that God commissioned those prophets to invite humanity to join together and form a society in submission to God's

28 Muhammad bin Jamil Zeno, *The Pillars of Islam and Iman* (Riyadh: Darussalam Publications, 1996), 30.

will/law. In the Islamic understanding of history, the peoples of the earth consistently rejected this invitation and God's prophets until God revealed the *Qur'an* through the prophet Muhammad. Many of these Muslim prophets are known to Christians as Adam, Noah, Abraham, Moses, David, Solomon… culminating in Jesus as the penultimate prophet, and finally the Prophet Muhammad as the seal of all prophets.[29] Islam teaches that Muhammad is the seal of Prophethood[30] because he was successful in communicating the message of God and establishing a society based on the revelation of the *Qur'an*. Islam also teaches that all of the prophets before Muhammad were rejected by the people, and the *Qur'an* was distorted by the few who incorrectly followed those prophets,[31] which explains for Muslims the existence of other scriptures. Therefore Muslims believe that the *Qur'an* as it is currently recited in Arabic today is the only scripture with true authority because it has been maintained in its pure Arabic form as it was revealed by God through the angel Gabriel to Muhammad, who then memorised and recited it successfully by God's help and power.

The two summary statements above are incomplete, of course. They should, however, begin to present just how differently Islam and Christianity understand the purpose and history of revelation, and the nature of Deity – and most important to this book, how all of that underpins and develops into two very different sets of religious and cultural value systems. For the vast majority of Muslims and Christians who are engaged in the daily interchange of life together for any reason, the differences between Christianity and Islam are experienced primarily in differing cultural values, often unconsciously, rather than in theological conversations. I

---

29 An excellent overview of the Islamic traditional view of these prophets can be found in: Ism a il ibn Umar Ibn Kathir, *Stories of the Prophets: Peace Be Upon Them*, 1st ed. (Riyadh: Darussalam, 1999).

30 In Islam, Prophets are divided into two classes according to their missions:
1. *Rasul* (lit. "Messenger", "Envoy"). A Prophet who brings a new religion or a major new revelation.
2. *Nabi* (lit. "Prophet"). A Prophet whose mission lies within the framework of an existing religion.
In Islam, prophethood has nothing to do with foretelling future events, only the delivery of God's revelation. see: *Glassé*, 364-5.

31 Please see Appendix 3 for a scholarly Islamic description of how the Christian and Jewish scriptures are corrupted and therefore without authority.

therefore highlight the importance of focusing on cultural values, because the differing theological foundations are expressed in everyday life through the cultural values they form. If we look carefully, we can actually see the root of theology in the culture.

For both Muslims and Christians, it is a person who lived in history and changed history, who defines our understanding of God; including God's character, purpose, and our appropriate response to his revelation. However, Jesus in Christianity and Muhammad in Islam cannot be directly compared to each other without thoroughly distorting their essential identities, and their respective roles as perceived by their followers.[32] Both religions revere their scriptures. However "pure" Islam and "pure" Christianity view the purpose and use of scripture very differently. In fact, Jesus is to Christians what the *Qur'an* is to Muslims. And the Bible is to Christians what the *Hadith* is for Muslims. The chart on the following page can clarify important considerations as we seek appropriate comparisons, and hopefully help us avoid inadvertent misrepresentations.

This diagrammatic text attempts to contrast Islamic and Christian understandings of the way in which Islam and Christianity perceive that revelation is received from God.

In Islam the *Qur'an*, which originated in Arabic according to most Muslims, pre-exists creation. When the *Qur'an* is recited (in Arabic) the Muslim hearer knows immediately that what is heard is nothing short of divine.[33] Consensus among Muslims proclaims that the poetry, flow and majesty of the language of the *Qur'an* could not have been composed by any human being. Of course the content is also considered revelatory, but non-Arabic speaking people cannot comprehend the power of the *Qur'an* because they cannot appreciate this dimension of transcendence in the language and poetry of the *Qur'an* itself, in comparison to any other Arabic literature. The form is as important as the content. Form and content together communicate the eternal divine origin of the *Qur'an* – the expression of God.[34]

---

32 Kenneth Cragg, *The Arab Christian: A History in the Middle East*, 1st ed. (Louisville, Ky.: Westminster/John Knox Press, 1991): 84.

33 Glassé, 267.

34 Hassan, Saab, 'Sacred and the profane in Islamic culture', *Journal of Religious Thought*, 20, 2 (1964): 147.

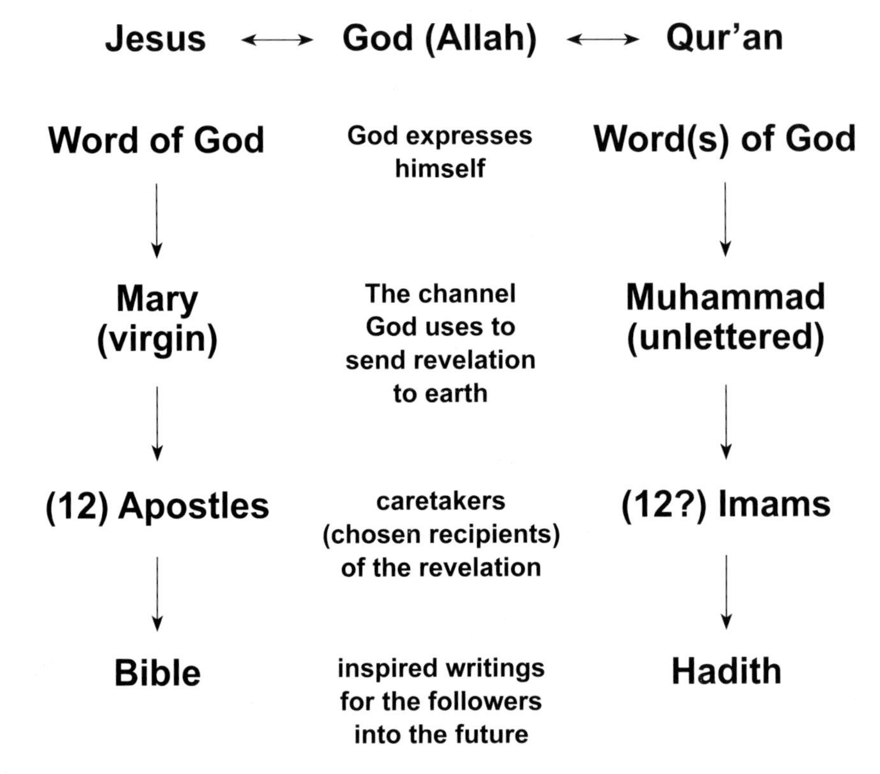

In Christianity Jesus, as the creative expression of God[35], exists before creation, activates creation in the beginning,[36] and becomes part of creation through a miraculous conception by the power of the Most High[37] and birth through Mary although she was a virgin. In this way, God reveals himself so that he can be known and reconciled to his creatures.[38] His followers, who

---

35 In Gen 1, God "said" *or* God "expressed himself." See also John 1:1-4 and Col 1:15-16. It is helpful to develop a dynamic/active understanding of the Greek term *Logos* as God's *expression* of himself rather than the common understanding associated with a person's title.

36 John 1:3.

37 Luke 1:35 *See also Surah 19:21 (Miriam); He said: "So (it will be): thy Lord saith 'That is easy for Me: and (We wish) to appoint him as a Sign unto men and a Mercy from Us': it is a matter (so) decreed."*

38 Heb 1:3a "He is the reflection of God's glory and the exact imprint of God's very being." (This concept is antithetical to the Islamic understanding of God's nature and purpose in revelation. God cannot be known. Associating any created being with God is the greatest of sins, known as *shirk*.)

were witnesses to these events and came to be known as apostles, carried this revelation to the world. Eventually those who followed this revelation collected the various writings of prophets and apostles that present the background and experience of this revelation – eventually compiled into a book, known to us as the Bible. To further clarify, Christian apostles are witnesses of the resurrection event, while Muslim apostles were tasked by God to recite/convey the *Qur'an*.

It should be noted that the comparison above between Muhammad and Mary can be sensitive. In the Islamic tradition Mary is revered, but she is not considered a prophet. In this diagram, the important focus is two-fold. First, God imparts revelation through a person. Traditional Islam would emphatically emphasise that Muhammad is *human*, a prophet like other prophets before him, except that Muhammad succeeded in his role where others had not. In fact, throughout history Muslims have proclaimed the miracle of the revelation of the *Qur'an* with the emphasis that Muhammad was not an educated man; many traditions would use the term 'illiterate'. This does not necessarily mean that Muhammad was unable to read and write, but that he was not a scholar – most specifically that he could not have been the composer of the *Qur'an*. The parallel in the diagram above with Mary is primarily presented in the sense that in Christianity Mary, as a virgin, miraculously gave birth to God's revelation in human expression which Christians understand to be Jesus; while Muhammad who was not a literate person "gave birth" to God's revelation in words which Muslims understand to be the *Qur'an*.

The diagram is an attempt to indicate the transmission – the flow – of revelation. In Islam, God entrusted the revelation of the *Qur'an* to various Muslim prophets throughout history. The *Qur'anic* word for "to reveal" *nazala* is to "send down". Muhammad is *the* prophet through whom the *Qur'an* was sent down, memorized and transmitted successfully. The personal followers of Muhammad[39] collected and wrote down his oral teachings after his death. Not only is the *Qur'an* preserved this way,

---

39 The early followers who became successors to Muhammad in leadership of the Islamic community are referred to as Imams. In modern usage, the person who leads prayers in the mosque and teaches the Islamic community is also referred to as an Imam. The usage is related but differently appointed.

but various proclamations of direction and guidance for right living and submission to God spoken verbally by Muhammad to his followers were also written down. This additional collection of sayings of the Prophet is revered as scripture and known collectively as the *Hadith*. Interpretation of the *Hadith* and the *Qur'an* together form the body of teaching known as the *Sunnah*, or *Shari 'a Law*. In Christianity, some who received the revelation of Jesus wrote down what they considered the essential message in his life and his teachings.[40] Additional writings of early followers of Jesus sought to express that revelation in broader cultural terms than the limitations of their historical Hebrew antecedent. Later these writings, in the Greek language, were collected and are revered together with the canon of Hebrew scripture which forms the historical context from which the revelation of Jesus came.

In simple terms, it can be demonstrated here that comparing Jesus and Muhammad, or comparing the Bible with the *Qur'an* is entirely inappropriate for Christians and Muslims who seek to comprehend each other's self-understanding. On a subtle level, comparing Jesus and Muhammad, the Bible with the *Qur'an* reinforces the Islamic view of the nature of revelation and implies that Christianity shares this view. More importantly, the contrast between God revealed as *transcendent* in Islam and God revealed as *immanent* in Christianity is more evident from this perspective as presented in the diagram. This distinction has far-reaching effects in the way the respective Islamic and Christian cultures perceive human responsibility, and the role of religion in the formation of social structures and human relationships. Most importantly, it should be clear that a Christian cannot understand Islam to any helpful degree as long as the context of her/his perception Islam is determined according to a Christian view of God and revelation. Obviously, the same is true in reverse for Muslims who are trying to understand Christianity.

The next chapter will help to explore how Christian and Muslim understandings of the nature of God also determine a different fundamental understanding of the purpose of what God has revealed and his intention in revealing.

---

40 Note the inclusion of both life and teaching, because both are revelatory. What Jesus did reveals God's love and nature every bit as much as what Jesus said.

3. THE PERCEPTION OF GOD

How (and how often) we speak about God inevitably influences our philosophical understanding of the relationship between the natural and supernatural, and our accountability to God as we perceive the nature of God. Personal habits and human interaction are inevitably influenced by our consciousness of God's presence and involvement in our lives.

The Arabic word 'Allah' is a contraction of *al-'ilāh*, literally translated as '*the Divinity*'.[41] In Arabic, and certainly in Islām, the vocabulary for God contains the definite article "the". There is a specificity and singularity inherent in the way Arabic-speaking people refer to God, which is conspicuously missing in the modern English usage "God". In Arabic, *Allah* is both the word for the conceptual idea of "godness" and the NAME of God. The Arabic, and Islam, retains an identification of God that Christians find familiar in the Old Testament references to Yahweh, the particular God of the Hebrew people, whose very name signifies his identity. *Allah* is God, unlike humanity – and separate from creation in every way. God is always greater; *Allah Akbar!*[42] "In Islam, the sacred is the wholly other, the One and Unique God, Allah. Islam is in a sense a passionate protest against attribution of sacredness to anyone or anything but Allah."[43] This specificity is subtle but it is a hugely important concept, contributing to the way Muslims have developed differing sets of cultural values from what is experienced in our secular American culture.

Calligraphy – "Allahu Akbar" (God is greater)

41 Glassé, 42.

42 Literally: "God is greater." This phrase introduces the call to prayer, and many other aspects of Islamic life. It is a constant reminder that the essence of *Allah* is 'other' than what can be perceived by his creatures. It is also the traditional battle cry of Muslims, signifying that *Allah* is the surety of victory and security of all Muslims.

43 Saab, 147.

It is essential to understand the influence of 18th century Deism as fundamental to the secularism inherent in the founding Fathers' formulation of the American legal framework. That influence continues to be thoroughly pervasive in American cultural attitudes.[44] While many Americans might accept the concept of 'intelligent design' in creation, or the philosophical existence of a Supreme Being, the culture no longer attributes personality (much less, relationship) to what has overwhelmingly and increasingly become a purely metaphysical concept of "God-ness".[45] The word "God" in common English usage no longer necessarily refers to a theistic, personal god. The New Oxford American Dictionary gives the second definition of GOD (after the particularly Christian reference) as "a superhuman being or spirit worshipped as having power over nature or human fortunes; a deity". The iconic phrase from the Star Wars[46] movies sums it up well; "May the Force be with you".

Americans, for instance, are comfortable speaking about a source of power, particularly power for goodness, but only "religious" people give much thought to what this means in everyday life. For example, the Alcoholics Anonymous designation of "a higher power"[47] has become a socially and culturally acceptable way to speak about Deity. For traditional Muslims however, "...God cannot be the First Cause or the Unmoved Mover of Aristotle. He is the Koranic God who is the Cause and Mover of everything."[48] For Muslims, *Allah* is not just the originator as creator, but existence only continues through *Allah's* daily management. While this doesn't seem very different from how many Christians who are intentional about their faith think about God, it *is* very different from how most people in Western society, including many Christians, apply the concept to daily life.

In Western culture, reality is most often defined by criteria of scientific

---

44 Robert D. Linder, 'Christianity, politics, and secular government in the United States', *Southwestern Journal of Theology*, 26, 2 (1984), 43, 53, 63.

45 Paul G Sonnack, 1984. "Church and state in light of the doctrine of the two kingdoms." *Word & World* 4, no. 3: 271.

46 The first film in the series was released on May 25, 1977, under the title *Star Wars*, by 20th Century Fox.

47 Step two of the twelve steps.

48 Saab, 115.

empiricism. 'Belief in a God' is considered unscientific at best or is regarded as simply foolish at worst.[49] Believing Christians are often challenged to "prove" the existence of God through some kind of empirical data or rational argument. It is hard to imagine where, in the Arab world,[50] one would read: "There is no distinction between believing in leprechauns, alien abductions, ESP, reincarnation or the existence of God – each equally lacks objective evidence."[51] That is not to disregard the prominence of *djinni*,[52] the "evil eye" and other supernatural phenomena within Islamic cultures, but more to attest that the supernatural is accepted as normal and needs no explanation or "proof" in Arab culture. There is no difficulty here for the Arab Muslim mind, which does not define rationality by empirical standards, but simply by what revelation, the *Sunnah*, says is true. God's presence is felt in every aspect of life. It is quite natural, therefore, for the Muslim culture to feature the name of God in jewellery design, calligraphic art, everyday speech, and behind every thought.

In Islamic culture God has "presence". Muslims are required to perform ritual ablutions before entering into the presence of God for prayer, and without the correct ritual in the ablution the prayer is considered void.[53] One must approach God with utmost reverence and respect. Although American culture held a similar sense of awe in an earlier age, increasing secularisation continues to erode the sense of reverence and recognition of God's influence in daily affairs. Even among Christians who are intentional about prayer and communion with God modern trends have increasingly de-emphasised ritual as an essential part of prayer and worship.[54] Islam

---

49 Mohammad Muhammad Zia Ullah, *Islamic Concept of God* (Boston: Kegan Paul International, 1984), 1.

50 Although there are millions of Arabic-speaking Christians in the 'Arab World' the underlying cultural habits are heavily influenced by the Islamic symbiosis with the Arab language and its everyday usages, both in word and in concept.

51 Quoted in: Massimo Pigliucci, 'Personal gods, deism, & the limits of skepticism', *Skeptic*, 8, 2 (2000): 44.

52 An intelligent spirit of lower rank than the angels. Generally, djinni (genies) are portrayed as mischievous in Arabic literature, rather than good or evil.

53 Mubarak Ali, *The Muslim Handbook* (Toronto: TSP, 2001) 12-15; Abdur Rahman Shad, *Muslim Etiquettes*, 1st ed. (Lahore: Kazi Publications, 1980) 81-91.

54 Paul F. M. Zahl, & Paul Basden. *Exploring the Worship Spectrum: 6 Views. Counterpoints* (Grand Rapids, Mich.: Zondervan, 2004), esp. 97-137.

maintains a clear sense of what is "clean/unclean,"[55] consistent with what Christians read in the Old Testament, which directs the believer in daily behaviour and habit. For example, it is very common for jewellery to feature the name of God (*Allah*) in the design, and there is a proscription followed by devout Muslim women to take off jewellery incorporating the name of *Allah* before entering a toilet area, because toilets are ritually unclean places.[56] To the Western mind practices like this seem to be silly superstition rather than a proper recognition of the seriousness that the Muslim mind applies to the sacred wonder of God's name, *Allah*. On the other hand, most Christians would understand, and often acknowledge, the same attribution of awe and serious attention to the name of God in Hebrew culture and tradition.

The ONENESS of God (*Tawheed*) is increasingly emphasised by Islamic purists[57] as "the utter exclusion of any analogy, similarity, or quality in creation that reflects or transmits God. This view of Tawheed is based upon dual negations within the *shahadah*[58] (There is *no god* except Allah). A complementary understanding of *Tawheed* is all-inclusive, that nothing is outside God. It is based upon the affirmation within the *shahadah* (there is no god *except Allah*). It is this latter view of *Tawheed* which predominates outside of fundamentalist movements today, and which certainly dominated Islam in the past."[59]

Calligraphy - 'Allah' (Arabic: the name of God)

It is important to clarify here that the apparent paradox between Islam's proclamation that God is utterly transcendent (unknowable) but at the same

55 See chapter 9 below.

56 Fu'ad ibn Abd al-Az iz Shalhub, *The Book of Manners*, 1st ed. (Riyadh: Darussalam, 2003), 232. Or Zeno, 58-59.

57 More and more characterised and led by the Wahabi subset of Hanbali Islam

58 Literally, 'witness'. The Islamic statement of faith, "There is no God but Allah, and Muhammad is the prophet of God."

59 Glassé, 453-454.

The Declaration of Faith (shahada)

لا إله إلا الله محمد رسول الله

"La ilaha illa Allah Muhammad Rasulu Allah"

Translation:

"There is no god but God, Muhammad is His Messenger"

Calligraphy representations of the 'Shahada', the Islamic statement of faith: There is no God but God and Mohammad is the Prophet of God

time he is seen to be ubiquitous in the daily affairs of life is no contradiction in Islam. To borrow a phrase from the apostle Paul's sermon on the aeropagus,[60] Muslims and Christians alike would affirm that 'in him we live, move, and have our being.' However, in Paul's sermon and in Islamic thought this phrase is more a statement of God's omnipresence, omnipotence, omniscience, et. al., rather than a reference to God's immanence. In fact, most Muslims would affirm all of the sermon up to the second half of verse 32. Believing Christians *can* see God's immanence in this sermon, but secular Americans could also read it in the same way Muslims do.

This cultural difference between the predominant vague American philosophical definition of Godness and the Islamic specificity presents a

60 Acts 17:22-31.

paradox to the believing Christian. It is not easy to identify with the Islamic presentation of God in so many ways, while at the same time recognising that God's identity is understood very differently in the traditions of the two different faiths. The indeterminate impersonal acceptance of a 'first cause' or 'higher power' in replacement of the incarnate revelation of God is repulsive to Muslims and thinking Christian alike. Conversely, the Incarnation is equally repulsive to secular Americans and Muslims alike, but for very different reasons. Muslims understand the nature of God as ultimately sovereign; *all that happens* must therefore be a manifestation of his will, or divine decree – very consistent with the characterisation of God as perceived in Old Testament history.[61] God is understood to be ever-present and directly involved in daily life, though perceived through his acts rather than his person.

In Islam the concept of "free will" and personal responsibility does not have the significance it carries in the Western analytical mind. Free will is attributed to God rather than humanity. "The sovereign free will of God affects every day of a person's life in the Muslim world. It includes the concept that God has complete power and can do whatever He wants to do. He has predestined every day of each person's life."[62] Traditional Muslims understand faith as self-submission to God's revelation in the *Sunnah*, as literally as possible.[63] Faith, in Islam, has nothing to do with intellectual assent/agreement with dogma. Faith in Islam is expressed in conforming to the will of God, who is "greater", greater than anything and all that could be imagined.

Because of this conviction, in Arab Islamic culture the concept of "God-ness" is perceived as power, not as person.[64] God's name (*Allah*) is

---

61 See: Num 16:28-32; Josh 10:10-13; 2 Kg 20:9-12.

62 Patrick O. Cate, 'Islamic Values and the Gospel', *Bibliotheca Sacra*,155, 619 (1998), 357.

63 Saab, 153.

64 Cate, 357. Islam utterly rejects the incarnational understanding of revelation; [4.171] *O People of the Book! Commit no excesses in your religion: Nor say of God aught but the truth. Christ Jesus the son of Mary was (no more than) an apostle of God, and His Word, which He bestowed on Mary, and a spirit proceeding from Him: so believe in God and His apostles. Say not "Trinity": desist: it will be better for you: for God is one God. Glory be to Him: (far exalted is He) above having a son. To Him belong all things in the heavens and on earth. And enough is God as a Disposer of affairs.*

Calligraphy representations of the 'Fatihah' invocation: In the name of God, the merciful, the compassionate.

pervasively mentioned in conversation. Speeches and journeys are begun by invoking the name and attributes of God.[65] All promises and plans are qualified with the caveat that fulfillment depends on the will of God.[66] Arabs – Muslim and Christian – are very comfortable including references to God in every aspect of conversation. Public acts of prayer and piety are not considered offensive. The call to prayer broadcast over loudspeakers five times every day is an ever present reminder that it is communal prayer and mutual submission to God that forms the very basis of social identity and coherence. In summary, the Islamic perception of God emphasises unity, mutuality, shared identity, and coherent society/community – while at the same time insisting that these expressions are only the appropriate human responses to God's revelation of the path for human social identity. It's

---

65 *"Bismillah Ir-Rahman Ir-Raheem"* **In the name of God, the merciful, the compassionate** is the appropriate opening to any speech, the beginning of a journey, and is often depicted in calligraphy in entrances to homes and businesses.

66 It is impossible to converse very long with an Arab Muslim without hearing the ubiquitous phrase, *Insha'Allah* which is most often translated, *God willing*.

Photo of a Shia mosque in Baghdad, Iraq

about how humans relate to each other and creation – not how we relate to God himself.

In American secular culture believing Christians can face difficulty in speaking publicly, especially in the workplace,[67] in ways which reflect matters of faith or their participation in church activities. Religion is increasingly relegated to the personal and private realm of life under programmes, and indeed in many cases legislation, designed to insulate education, commerce, sport and politics from religious influences. Among a large segment of American society it is no longer considered appropriate to refer to God as a "player" in the daily life of society. Religion is understood to equate with philosophy rather than with lifestyle. In this light, we should not be surprised to read or learn that Arab Muslims perceive, along with many conservative American Christian writers, Western culture as godless and spiritually bankrupt.[68] In societies where moral and ethical standards are no longer defined by any religious standard but rather increasingly defined simply by majority opinion, believing Christians are no longer accustomed to hearing the name of God in conversation, other than in the use of expletives!

The secular idea that religion is strictly a personal, individualistic and private choice/preference is inconceivable in the Arab world, even among Arab Christians, whereas most Americans have been influenced by the social convention that it is impolite to bring up politics and religion in conversation and it is socially incorrect to assume that religious values are shared. Unfortunately, in the interaction between Islamic and Western cultures these very different value systems influence significant mutual misconceptions between the peoples who make up the two different cultures. Secular Westerners often and readily conclude that Muslims

---

67 Consider, for example, the controversy in recent years over the use of "Merry Christmas" in retail outlets. See: Richard K. Olsen, and Julie W. Morgan, "Happy Holidays: creating common ground in the 'war on Christmas', *Journal of Religion and Popular Culture*, 21, no. 3 (September 1, 2009): *ATLA Religion Database with ATLASerials*, EBSCO*host* (accessed December 28, 2013). For a survey of legal cases regarding religious expression in the workplace see: Brown, Steven P. 'Leaving the spiritual sphere: religious expression in the public workplace', *Journal of Church and State*, 49, 4 (2007): 665-682.

68 Yvonne Yazbeck Haddad, 'Muslim revivalist thought in the Arab world: an overview', *Muslim World*, 76, no. 3-4 (1986), 147.

are religious fanatics. Many Muslims conclude that although American culture offers prosperity and opportunity, it is essentially a godless culture. Americans who are new to living in Arab society, for instance, are often intimidated with the very public way Muslims and Arab Christians integrate religious piety, habits and values into every facet of daily life. However, it must be remembered that piety is essentially an expression of religious culture, or subculture, and not necessarily reflective of any personal connection with God.

As mentioned in a previous chapter, Christians believe that in Jesus God is reconciling all of creation to himself. Christians believe that God's intention in creation reflects his character of love and as desirous of relationship. Because Christians understand God to offer us covenant, we presume an inherent obligation on God's part to fulfill his promises, to forgive repentant sinners, and Christians perceive God's nature as unchanging. In Islam, God does not engage in covenant or relationship with creation. Because God is perceived as so completely transcendent or "other" there is no thought to understanding God's nature,[69] or expectations attributed to God's interaction with creation.[70] It is not unusual for Muslims to talk about God as if he is capricious and for that attribution to be regarded as a manifestation of God's sovereignty. The Biblical idea that God could be accountable to any human completely contradicts the Islamic view of God's nature as ultimately sovereign. "Since the *Qur'an* portrays the human predicament as primarily ignorance rather than evil, as in the biblical analysis, the Muslim sees only the need of a guide, not a saviour."[71]

All that being said, it is not difficult to see why some Christians are attracted to the popular evangelical literature proposing that Muslims worship a different God than Christians do. Aside from the obvious contradiction that a professing monotheistic Christian would entertain the idea that two

---

69 Ansari, 433, 435.

70 Cate, 357.
Glassé, 220. God in Islam is known under the aspect of eternity, without commitments in history, neither 'repenting' nor sending down 'a son', always returning to His Absoluteness, and seen from the abstract of metaphysics rather than as a participant in a religious drama shared with his creation.

71 Woodberry, 177.

different gods actually exist, one Christian and another Muslim, this trend is indicative of the inability of many Christians to appreciate that many Muslims believe that Christians are polytheists,[72] and how this particular modern trend unfortunately reinforces that conviction. The recently re-popularised proposal that Islam and Christianity worship two different gods is only one example. Does not this idea presume a polytheistic conviction?[73] From a purely linguistic perspective, there is no room to entertain this approach to explain away the differences between Islam and Christianity.

> Etymologically, Jews, Christians and Muslims originally called God by virtually identical names. The Arabic All_h comes from the same root as the biblical "God" (El_hîm, h_-El_hîm and h_-Elôh) invoked by the Hebrew prophets or the Aramaic/Syriac Al_h_ presumably used by John the Baptist and Jesus. Historically, we have identified our "object of worship" – probably the literal proto-Semitic sense of All_h, El_hîm, and Al_h_ – as the God of Abraham.[74]

Indeed, the Islamic and Christian perception of revelation, and therefore the perception of the nature of God is very different, but negating the difference by avoiding it will not help Christians understand Islam – or represent Christian faith appropriately.

Because the very essence of Islam and the meaning of the word itself is bound up in submission to God it is easy for many Christians to equate the Christian concept of obedience to God with Islamic submission to the *Sunnah*. Herein lies a critical distinction; obedience to God who reveals his

---

72 *Surah* 4:171. *O People of the Book! Commit no excesses in your religion: Nor say of Allah aught but the truth. Christ Jesus the son of Mary was (no more than) an apostle of Allah, and His Word, which He bestowed on Mary, and a spirit proceeding from Him: so believe in Allah and His apostles. Say not "Trinity": desist: it will be better for you: for Allah is one Allah. Glory be to Him: (far exalted is He) above having a son. To Him belong all things in the heavens and on earth. And enough is Allah as a Disposer of affairs.*

73 Miroslav Volf's argument covers this concept comprehensively. "If the argument were good, Christians would have to say that the God of the Jews is false, and the Catholic Christians would be forced to say that the God of Orthodox Christians is false, and so on. Miroslav Volf, *Allah: A Christian Response* (New York, Harper Collins, 2011), 188

74 Umar F. Abd-Allah, 'Do Christians and Muslims worship the same God?', *Christian Century*, 121, 17 (2004), 34.

'self' in the incarnation is very different from submission to law, even law emanating from God himself. This, of course, is the substance of debate in Romans 3. Christians are habitually distracted by the tension between law and grace. Through the revelation of God in human form, Jesus, we find forgiveness, reconciliation and relationship in God rather than a set of rules for right living.

Muslims and Christians alike find that they struggle with moral standards, definitions of righteousness and sin. Obedience and right living are goals for forms of piety in religious practice as well as in modalities of worship. The next chapter will offer some perspective on personal and corporate 'striving' to live to the fullness of the revelation of God as we perceive it.

4. Jihad & Ijtihad[75]

O man! surely you must strive (to attain) to your Lord, a hard striving until you meet Him. Surah 84:6

They believe in Allah and the last day, and they enjoin what is right and forbid the wrong and they strive with one another in hastening to good deeds, and those are among the good. Surah 3:114

Most Americans associate the word "*Jihad*" with violence and terrorism. It is indeed true that there are different Islamist groups who specifically identify with the *Al Qa'eda* movement, some even calling themselves *Islamic Jihad*. Even so, the concept of *jihad* is very broad and has many meanings/ usages among Muslims. Without an informed understanding of *jihad* there is little hope of coming to a comfortable and practical understanding of Islam, especially since the word is so fundamental to Islamic theology. To give us a starting point, let us consider how the concept of *jihad* is practised in Christianity.

Among practising Christians the discipline of daily devotions and reading of scripture is understood to be a good thing for nurturing one's faith. From a strictly doctrinal perspective, this personal effort is not 'necessary' to achieve salvation because salvation is a gift through the merits of Jesus Christ. The practice of daily devotions can be more appropriately understood as an attitude and discipline that enables the individual Christian to benefit more fully from that grace and gift provided by God in Christ. Certainly, among our secular friends this kind of daily discipline is often interpreted as excessive or even fanatic. It even sounds excessive to many who attend weekly worship, much to the frustration of many pastors! The same dilemma applies to the Islamic understanding of *jihad*, which is appropriately understood as an effort to nurture one's full submission to God.

Differences in lifestyle and values between secular-minded, non-religious people and intentionally-religious people, regardless of their faith tradition, are often easy distinctions to make. However, among the more fervent practitioners of any faith there is often a scale of commitment to, and

---

75 From Arabic *jihād*, literally 'effort,' expressing, in Muslim thought, struggle on behalf of God and Islam.

definition of, devotional practice. An indicator of the spectrum between simple personal intentionality or imposing fanaticism could be seen in the degree in which a particular person or group insists that his/her personal understanding of the faith should be the standard for others within the same faith tradition or, not insignificantly, by all people universally. Perhaps in thinking of this scale we can more aptly apply concepts that help us grasp the concept of *jihad.*

Modern Christians, especially Evangelicals, use the word 'crusade' with a great variety of meanings. Of course everyone knows the origin of the word which refers to a series of invasions and war between people in Europe and people in the Levant[76] during the Middle Ages. In spite of the religious fervour on both sides that characterised the movement, any casual student of history can readily see that politics, economics and ethnocentrism were also strong motivational foundations to the various Crusades which took place during the 11th-13th centuries. Only uninformed people in modern times could look back on this period in European history purely as a religious movement.[77] Nevertheless, the word 'crusade' cannot *not* have a religious connotation. And so, during the past half-century, the word has often been appropriated for imagery in a broad spectrum of programmes for strengthening or expanding Christian influence. 'Crusade' can refer to a series of presentations in a local church, or a global missionary movement dedicated to convert all people to a particular interpretation of Christian tradition – and everything in between (including non-religious "crusades" to end poverty, crime, and malaria!) In the Middle East, the word is often invoked to decry any kind of (particularly Western) foreign influence that threatens the continuity of accepted social, economic, cultural or religious values. In short, the word has many meanings variously understood as positive or negative in application. In Western culture, particular within Church culture, it is most often employed as a positive image while in the

---

76 The eastern part of the Mediterranean, including present day Cyprus, Israel, Jordan, Lebanon, Palestine, and Syria.

77 Carole Hillenbrand, 'The Islamic World and the Crusades', *Scottish Journal of Religious Studies*, 7, no. 2 (September 1, 1986), 151. See also: Evan S. Connell, *Deus Lo Volt!: Chronicle of the Crusades* (Washington, D.C.: Counterpoint, 2000); Francesco Gabrieli, *Arab Historians of the Crusades* (London: Routledge & Kegan Paul, 1969); Amin Maalouf, *The Crusades through Arab Eyes* (London: Al Saqi, 1984).

Middle East it is universally negative.[78]

It is helpful to understand the Islamic term *jihad* in much the same way. The primary historic association with the word describes what is commonly called the Arab Conquest, the astonishingly rapid militaristic expansion of Islam into the Levant and across northern Africa, while spreading east through Persia and reaching into India. Religious fervour underlying the conquest is today understood by Muslims to be an indication of God's blessing on the then new revelation of Islam.

Over the centuries since, increasing emphasis has been given to personal religious efforts to enhance individual submission to God, to call others to submission to God, the purification of Islamic society from deviant behaviour, and among groupings of Muslims who work to eradicate non-Islamic influences within the process of social evolution.[79] For example, Arab Muslim charities are funding schools and mosques all over the world in non-Islamic countries. This effort (*jihad*) to build places of nurture for Muslims is similar to Christian mission schools built in India or Africa to ensure that the minority Christian population can educate children according the Christian values. Could not this form of *jihad* also be compared to contemporary programmes sponsored by Evangelical Christians in America for returning America to her Christian roots?

Ijtihad is a somewhat refined variant on the concept of 'effort' on behalf of Islam. Where *jihad* is most often understood as practical effort in the extension of Islam[80] or other efforts that relate to the Islamic community, *ijtihad* is used most often in respect to how Muslims view and apply faith to life. The most common use of the term *ijtihad* relates to the work of interpreting the *Sunnah* for personal or community life. On one level, it represents personal endeavor to apply knowledge of custom and tradition

78 During the 1991 Gulf War Muslim nationalists characterised the Desert Storm operation as a modern crusade. The 19th century missionary movement in the Middle East is also often referred to by Muslims as a modern crusade. In addition, the colonial/imperialist movement of European powers is also described as a "second wave" of the old Crusades. Even Communist efforts to gain political influence in the Middle East during the latter half of the 20th century is often called a crusade. Of course, the most pervasive and dramatic modern association with the original Crusader movement is Zionist success in the Holy Land itself.

79 Haddad, 155.

80 Muslims are also engaged in evangelism, so to speak.

to new experience in life. The main emphasis, however, is a scholarly debate attempting to relate Islamic precepts to an ever-changing world. This process gave rise to a comprehensive and somewhat complex system of Islamic jurisprudence in the early centuries of Islam, which continues today. Increasing social changes spurred by technology and modernity bring special problems to *ijtihad.*

As a systematic endeavour to apply revelation to daily life in a changing world, Islamic jurisprudence is sacred. Its continuing development is a 'striving' to guide society and the Islamic faithful in the ways of God. This body of jurisprudence is called *Shari'a* today. Al Ghazali, an 11th century theologian and jurist whom some consider the most influential Muslim in history after Muhammad, defines the objective of *Shari'a* as follows:

> They are protecting the five essential values, namely life (*al-nafs*), religion and faith (*iman*), intellect and reason (*eaql*), lineage (*nasi*), and property (*mal*). All legal rules and any legal system must secure these values and all measures that secure these values and interests fall within the scope of *maslahah*, and anything which violates them is *mafsadah* (corruption).[81]

During the post-colonial era of 1950-1970, many Islamic countries struggled to define their nationalism in opposition to Islamic religious and cultural roots, as well as modern education and urban industrialised economies, and particularly the influence of secularism. There is great emphasis on returning to *Shari'a* as a way of holding onto Islamic identity in an ever-changing world.[82] Americans would find echoes of this trend in "Back to the Bible" movements in the USA.

Conservative Muslims, on the other hand, abide by a widely-held tradition in Islam that the door to *ijtihad* was closed in the 11th century CE. This conviction is based on the belief that scholars are now too far removed from the purity of Islam for a reliable interpretation of the Prophet's life and intentions. This belief/policy has created a dilemma within Islamic society

---

81 A. Ezzati, 'Islamic law and the challenges of modern times', *Journal of Shi'a Islamic Studies*, 3, 1 (2010), 47.

82 Fred Halliday, 'The Politics of the Umma: States and Community in Islamic Movements', *Mediterranean Politics,* 7, 3 (2002), 36.

between those seeking to 'modernise' Islam and those who are convinced that a return to the roots of Islam is needed to ensure that Muslims fulfil their mandate from God.[83] This dilemma is not dissimilar to current trends among Evangelicals throughout the world. While some are striving to reinterpret sacred texts in light of social development, particularly in regard to sexuality and feminism, others are convinced that a return to traditional interpretation of scripture and 'family values' will bring security to society and coherence to our religious identity. However, because Islamic social interaction is more comprehensively defined by *Shari'a*, this 'striving' has developed a more polarised reaction to modernity among Muslims and, significantly, contributed to an increasing expression of fundamentalism.[84]

It should be relatively clear that both individuals and whole societies in modern times are struggling to balance the way values are defined, and how one or another sub-group in any society may or may not impose its own values onto the general society as a whole. The next chapter will explore how personal and public identity is understood in Islamic society, and why it is different than what is experienced in the West.

---

83 Sherifa Zuhur, *Revealing Reveiling: Islamist Gender Ideology in Contemporary Egypt* (New York: State University of New York Press, 1992), 14.

84 Osama Abi-Mershed, 'Degrees of interpretive autonomy: ijtihād and the constraints of competence and context in late medieval Tilimsan', *Islam and Christian-Muslim Relations*, 13, 2 (2002), 152

5. PERSONAL AND PUBLIC IDENTITY

Muslims do not wrestle with the concept of guilt, of a legal sin, of doing something that is wrong before God. Instead they wrestle with the concept of shame, of bringing dishonor to one's family or to oneself. They are concerned with what people would say or what people would think. The preservation of self-respect is of the highest value.[85]

Perhaps the most difficult aspect of Islamic culture for Christians to grasp is the dynamic tension between personal and public identity. When an American is asked to tell about him/herself, the answer will likely focus on one's profession, lifestyle preferences, sport interest or hobbies. Arab Muslims will almost always focus his/her response based on his/her place in clan/family and the family's status in society, family origin, and some historic references that are felt to give substance to the family identity. In other words, individuality is not the defining aspect of identity in Islamic culture as it is in Western society. This difference is derived from the different understandings relating to God's purpose in revelation, the identity of God and how the two different societies comprehend the appropriate human response to God's revelation. Although this may not seem remarkable it has far-reaching implications in the daily routines of life. Personal responsibility, personal decisions, and willingness to try something new are all greatly influenced by the way a person's identity is reflected in society.

We have already touched upon the value that Americans, in particular, place on individuality. We have also explored the Islamic value of *Tawheed*, (unity) – a society of people mutually submitted to God's guidance as revealed in the *Sunnah*.[86] For instance, the Western sense that society has an obligation to protect the rights of the individual presents a direct contrast with the Islamic sense of the individual's relationship with society.

> From an Islamic perspective, personal and moral autonomy (whether based on theories of rights or on Kantian individualism) is a kind of nonsense, for two reasons: first, it involves usurping God's

---

85 Cate, 368.

86 Halliday, 25.

own position as the judge of good and evil; and second, it cuts the individual off from the community of faith. Goodness is not just an individual matter in Islam, as we have seen, and society has a duty to publicly uphold.[87]

The way we understand the use of words like "autonomy" and "individuality" are important if we want to understand why Muslims and Christians hold very different values about personal and public identity. Because Western culture has grown out of Christian culture, the idea of personal moral responsibility to God and community suggests that society is made up of individuals and social identity is determined democratically by the collective will of the people. Conversely, Islamic morality says that individual identity is derived, determined and managed by extended family/society.[88]

Most Westerners who live in Arab societies are significantly challenged by the lack of emphasis on individuality and personal initiative/choice. For Westerners, traditional customs in Muslim societies like arranged marriages and social mandates about appropriate dress are perceived as an affront to the personal freedom of the individual.[89] And that 'freedom of the individual' is exactly the point of divergence between the two sets of social values. Americans and Europeans place considerable emphasis on individuality/autonomy. Personal initiative is encouraged from a very young age, and admired by society. Islamic values present a stark contrast; "Rather than thinking of individual rights and making decisions as individuals, the consensus of the community makes decisions for its members."[90] Because the Muslim individual's identity is defined by family and society, he/she is ever conscious of how decisions, actions, choices will affect social identity and how he/she will be perceived by the family and social network.

---

87 J Mark Halstead, 'Islamic values: a distinctive framework for moral education?', *Journal of Moral Education*, 36, 3 (2007), 289.

88 David D Grafton, 'The Arab Shaykh: Authority in Christian and Muslim Communities, and Questions of Social-Political Reform', *Islam and Christian-Muslim Relations*, 23, 1 (2012), 24.

89 It should be remembered that arranged marriages are still the norm among Christians in many countries and proscribed standards of dress exist among Christians in the United States.

90 Cate, 364.

Privacy, as well, is a very strong value in Western society. From a very young age Americans are taught to "mind your own business", and actually believe that their personal choices and actions do not necessarily affect others around them. Of course social responsibility and accountability is assumed and encouraged, but it is very clear that civic responsibility is a matter of choice even while at the same time it is promoted as a duty. The default understanding of democracy enshrines the state's responsibility to uphold the rights and privileges of the citizen/individual more than the individual's responsibility toward society.[91] Islamic society perceives this important secular value as rebellion against God's law; the idea that an individual is encouraged to make choices at all denies the sovereignty of God, who has decreed the correct behaviour for all in society.[92]

Returning to the concept of *Tawheed*, it is important to emphasise that coherence and integration are essential in Islamic society. In Islam individuality is, by definition, counter-intuitive to the character of social identity. Just as the *Qur'an* is the standard for the Arabic language, imitation of the Prophet is the standard for Islamic behaviour and relationships.[93] Muslims orient their personal values and personal habits, and even personal hygiene in imitation of the Prophet, in accordance with the *Hadith*.

Manners and etiquette, the second dimension of moral behaviour, clearly extend the concept of morality beyond what is normally included in western understandings of the term. Because of the reverence in which the Prophet Muhammad is held in Islam, every small detail of his personal lifestyle and behaviour becomes a model for Muslims, including how he ate food and drank, how he prepared for bed, what side he slept on, how he washed, how he relieved himself, how he dyed his hair, how he responded to sneezing and yawning, how he acted in the presence of his wives. This is the main reason why the collections of *hadith* are so important, because by providing a record of what the Prophet did and said, they simultaneously provide a guide to Muslims about how to behave. It is therefore rare to find any debate about family values or sexual values in Islam, because these matters

91 Grafton, 28.

92 Tahmina Rashid, 'Secular State, Citizenship and the Matrix of Globalized Religious Identity', *Alternatives: Turkish Journal of International Relations*, 6, no. 1&2 (2007), 158

93 Halstead, 284.

are resolved by reference to the words and actions of the Prophet.[94]

In Islamic tradition there has been little motivation to analyse the reasons why Muhammad did or said any particular thing. Because his life is regarded as the model for all believers, imitating the Prophet is the standard for all Muslims in determining behavioural values. "Therefore, unlike other revealed religions, the fundamental tenets of Islam (i.e., the five pillars) are not debated as they were interpreted and 'tested' by Muhammad, who is also referred to as 'The Walking *Qur'an*.'"[95] Imitating Muhammad and following his advice is regarded as the perfect way to live. And therefore, as Muslims individually strive to conform their values, behaviour and social interactions in imitation of the life of the Prophet, they are naturally and mutually conforming to each other, contributing to a comprehensive unity in the society.

Because Arab Muslims derive their identity from their social relationships[96] morality is defined in the context of relationships between people, rather than between the person and God. The *Sunnah* presents very detailed rules of behaviour and interactions between members of society, rather than between humans and God.[97] Because these rules are religious in nature, Westerners often presume these rules pertain to the Muslim's relationship with God. However, it is inaccurate to impose what is essentially a Christian understanding of scripture and Christian faith on Islam as a religion or as a society. Christians naturally presume that these Islamic rules are about "right and wrong", because we look to scriptures to define our relationship with a covenant God.[98] In Islam God is not perceived to be offering covenant; the Islamic scriptures are about right social relationships rather than the way people relate to God. Christians think of sin as an offence against God; Muslims understand sin as deviation from God's revealed law for guiding human society. Christians are concerned about individual moral choices; Muslims are concerned to create a society that expresses and conforms to

---

94 Halstead, 288.

95 Carolyn Ball, "Diversity in Religious Practice: Implications of Islamic Values in the Public Workplace" *Public Personnel Management* vol. 32 no. 3 (Fall 2003), 317.

96 Grafton, 23.

97 Halstead, 284.

98 Cate, 365.

God's revelation.

A key concept for the Christian to grasp is the Islamic, particularly Arab Islam, sense of being a *chosen* community.

> *Ye*[99] *are the best of peoples, evolved for mankind, enjoining what is right, forbidding what is wrong, and believing in God. Surah 3:110a*
>
> *They were, in our sight, truly, of the company of the Elect and the Good. Surah 38:47*

These verses from the *Qur'an*, among others, confirm to Muslims that they, as a society, have been appointed a pivotal role in the world and in history. Muslims *witness* to the unity of God and the message given through his prophet through the way their prayers and their social customs, their consciousness of the Islamic community, and through their prosperity[100] and understanding of dominion all express a sense of unified community. The moral standards for society that Islam proclaims are understood to be nothing less than the will of God.

> Above all we must be firmly convinced, with complete faith and enthusiasm, that we have a scheme of life greater than any possessed by the followers of any religion or school or civilisation that yet been born, because it is the product of God, the creator of life.[101]

All of this is not dissimilar to the Jewish self-understanding that we find in the Old, and New Testament with the incredibly important difference that the ancient Jews understood that their covenant with Yahweh was for Jews alone, while Islam understands that the revelation given to Muhammad is for the world. Muslims are extremely conscious of the image they project to each other and to the world outside the *House of Islam*. Because Muslims are ever-conscious of their communal identity, and the honour of Islam itself, behavioural criteria are different from those in secular society. "The familiar western binary oppositions of 'right' and 'wrong', 'good' and 'bad'

---

99 It might be helpful here to note that the 'ye' is plural, and certainly not individualistic.

100 Many Muslims interpret prosperity, given by God of course, as a sign of his particular favour upon Muslims. This is not unlike the preaching observed among many Pentecostal Christian churches of course.

101 Sayyid Qutb, *Social Justice in Islam*. Rev. ed. (Oneonta, N.Y.: Islamic Publications International, 2000), 284.

do not fully capture the moral distinctions that are fundamental to Islam."[102] Muslims are more tuned to the contrast of shame/honour than to an abstract sense of sense of right/wrong. I don't mean to say here that right/wrong values are unimportant in Islam. The point here is that shame/honour is a more consciously contrasting motivational criteria among Muslims in their social relationships.

Stories abound of Arab women visiting the aircraft lavatory on flights arriving in Gulf countries to don their *abayas* before the plane begins to land; or, of Muslims drinking alcohol when none of their friends can see them; or a Muslim man's attitude about his German wife's style of dress changing when they move from Germany back to his homeland. These and other stories are indications of the essential role of the communal identity in the life of the individual in Islamic culture. When Westerners perceive these attitudes as hypocrisy, they are evaluating the situation with criteria based on fundamentally Western/European historical understandings of behaviour and morality, integrity and consistency. Because Islamic culture focuses much more heavily on social coherence rather than individual morality, individual behaviour is governed by values like conformity and approval. Because Arab Muslims are 'tuned' to think in terms of Islamic dignity and honour, respect for one's family and one's family reputation in society is of the utmost importance. Individual behaviour is driven by a desire for approval among the extended family, particularly elders, while any behaviour that brings shame on the self, the family, or disapproval of the elders, is to be avoided. Individual behaviour away from home, which does not reflect on the honour of the family, is diminished in significance.

Increasing media attention focused on the *hijab*, or head cover for Muslim women, is another case in point. Western media generally approaches the subject in the context of women's rights. For many Muslim women, the *hijab* is indeed a symbol of women's rights – the right to wear the symbol of their religion even in non-Muslim countries. In fact, though many Muslim scholars admit that the *hijab* is not mandated in the *Sunnah*, over the last generation it has become synonymous with Islamic piety.[103] In practice, this

---

102 Halstead, 287.

103 Zuhur, 74, 78.

means that there is social pressure on Muslim women to 'cover'; otherwise they can be judged by peers as impious. In the past 50 years the *hijab* has become a symbol of identity and commitment to Islam, and Islamic values. One comparison would be the pride/determination with which a Christian woman would visibly wear a cross in a workplace where co-workers are known to disparage Christians and Christianity.

Another credible parallel that can lend understanding to this phenomenon would be to recall the popularity of displaying national flags at homes, on cars, as stickers on schoolbooks, etc. in the months after the 9/11 tragedy. Communal affirmation is not the same thing as peer pressure. For an Arab Muslim woman, refusal to 'cover' can be seen as rebellion against the standards of the family, or even society in general in some countries. Conversely, those who cover receive approval and encouragement from their peers. It is important here to note that in this perspective the *hijab* is primarily a matter of social identity, a statement of promoting a particular society and its values – and consequent rejection of others. *In this context* the hijab is definitely NOT a symbol of male oppression, but of identity, pride and honour.

With these concepts of personal and public identity in mind, we shall move on to examine ways in which personal choices are reflected in respect to personal and public responsibility.

6. CHOICES AND PERSONAL RESPONSIBILITY

In Islamic law Muslims are told they are their brother's keeper, and they are responsible to use whatever is necessary to keep other Muslims from doing wrong. In the West, Christians say each person must individually choose to follow Christ. But in Islam, individual thinking is not valued. Group pressure is exerted against those who would consider anything other than Islam. Pressure from one's community and family encourages each Muslim to think and act in accord with Islamic values.[104]

One of the defining characteristics of the kind of Protestantism that influenced the formation of Western secular culture is the conviction that for faith to be efficacious, it must be personally appropriated and expressed. Although this is a specific focus of the Reformation/Evangelical tradition in Christianity, the same principle is basic to all Christians to varying degrees of implicit or explicit awareness. Within different Protestant traditions, there is an assumption that life 'in Christ' will somehow lead to "righteousness" "sanctification" "election" etc. This is expressed in daily life in the belief that *all* personal choices reflect personal moral values, a sense of either right or wrong; believing Christians would speak about it in terms of righteousness or sin. Another way to express this principle is to say that personal choices reflect a person's understanding of their relationship with God. Concurrently, for believing Christians a direct correlation to this principle is a presupposition that no person is perfect, and that sin is an inherent component of human nature, but that God in his goodness has provided a means of salvation through the life, death and resurrection of Jesus Christ. All of these considerations reflect a world-view rooted in Christian tradition and values. In the encounter with Islam, though, one must learn to think differently.

Christians who wish to engage with Muslims in fruitful interaction, whether in religious contexts or simply in the workplace, will communicate more effectively if they understand that Islam has no

---

104 Cate, 365.

context for the Christian concept of personal salvation: that the Islamic perspective for sin has no sense of an abstract moral 'right and wrong.'[105] Islam defines sin as "an act of disobedience to God's law, a breaking of moral and social conventions."[106] While on the surface this may seem consistent with much in Christian teaching, the operative words here are the reference to *moral and social conventions*. The Islamic concept of sin is not rooted in man's individual relationship with God, but man's relationship with society. Western Christians will interact with Muslims more comfortably when they understand that in Islam sin is viewed more in terms of *deviant* behaviour rather than as *immoral* behaviour. It is also important to note that in Islam, sin has nothing to do with the human nature, but only human behaviour.

> Muslims do not wrestle with the concept of guilt, of a legal sin, of doing something that is wrong before God. Instead they wrestle with the concept of shame, of bringing dishonour to one's family or to oneself. They are concerned with what people would say or what people would think. The preservation of self-respect is of the highest value.[107]

When something goes wrong in the workplace, or in a relationship, necessitating some level of reconciliation or recovery, it is unhelpful to assume that a Muslim colleague understands our particular Christian/Western idea of right and wrong, morality and immorality. It must be remembered that these values are an outgrowth of our Christian heritage and the Christian definitions of sin and righteousness. "Their concern before God is not to find forgiveness, but to submit to whatever He has decided. Submission to God is a crucial core value of Islam."[108] Let us explore the theological underpinning of this aspect of Arab Islamic culture before looking at how it is worked out in daily life.

For Muslims, it is almost preposterous to consider that an individual human's choices or behaviour could have any bearing on God.

---

105 Cate, 368.

106 Chapman, 27.

107 Cate, 368.

108 Cate, 358.

It is not fitting for a believer, man or woman, when a matter has been decided by God and His Apostle, to have any option about their decision; if any one disobeys God and His Apostle, he is indeed on a clearly wrong Path. (Surah 33:36)

God is wholly transcendent, other, unknowable, not connected to humanity – except that in his goodness he has given decrees for the benefit of human society. "God is without limits, without dimensions. We would be fools to ask for Him to step down from His throne of infinite attributes to become comprehensible for us. How can a limitless, infinite being be contained in the mind of a limited being like man?"[109] Muslims see temptation as a struggle ordained by God, as a testing process. The outcome has no bearing on God himself – only on the person's awareness of his/her submission to God's will.[110] Looking at this from within a Christian understanding of God it is important to note that in Islam the struggle between good and evil relates to God's commandments rather than to God himself. This is not only important in respect to an attempt to understand Islam theologically, but it figures in human/social relationship as expressed in business, sport, social events, academic pursuits, and everything else in which Christians and Muslims interact in everyday life.

Islamic piety ubiquitously but deeply expressed in the phrase "*in sha allah*"[111] is largely misunderstood by non-Muslims. For many non-Arabs living in the Middle East, the use of this phrase can be misperceived as an excuse to avoid responsibility for decisions or commitments, or being late for an appointment. This misunderstanding is borne out of a failure

---

109 Ullah, 19.

110 Bernard Lewis, "The roots of Muslim rage" *Atlantic Monthly* 266, no. 3: 47-54 (1990), 49.

111 Most often translated as "If God wills" or "God Willing", it is not dissimilar to the Western literary tradition of inscribing D.V. (Deus Volente), meaning "God Willing" at the end of a letter, or other text. This piety in Islam is based on *Surah* 18:23-24: *"And do not say of anything: Surely I will do it tomorrow, unless Allah pleases; and remember your Lord when you forget and say: Maybe my Lord will guide me to a nearer course to the right than this."* and the same piety in Christian cultural tradition can be recognized in James 4:13-15: Come now, you who say, "Today or tomorrow we will go to such and such a town and spend a year there, doing business and making money." Yet you do not even know what tomorrow will bring. What is your life? For you are a mist that appears for a little while and then vanishes. Instead you ought to say, "If the Lord wishes, we will live and do this or that.

to comprehend the Islamic focus on God as completely transcendent. This phrase, interjected at all points of conversation which considers a future event or development, or an outcome not yet determined, points to the conviction that God (Allah) directs our lives, not we ourselves. Many Muslims would ascribe great presumption to the non-Muslim who promises to meet the next day at a particular time without acknowledging that it is really up to God whether or not the meeting will take place. In fact, *in sha allah* is more properly understood as, "I'll meet you tomorrow (*bukra*) at ten o'clock, *in sha allah*.[112] While many devout Christians would also nod in assent to the principle that our lives are in God's hands, the concept of *free will* imposes a high degree of personal responsibility. For most people from Western countries, *free will* inherantly means freedom to make one's own choices. While this freedom to choose implies freedom even to ignore God and his ways, in Christian theology it also implies an invitation to participate with God in the stewardship of creation through obedience and submission.[113] These concepts are incomprehensible in an Islamic world view. *Islam*, meaning submission, presumes that the role of humanity in relation to God is only submission, certainly not participation. That level of familiarity with God would be considered *Shirk!*[114]

Calligraphy – "in sha Allah" (if God wills)

Another example, in keeping with the use of the phrase "*in sha allah*", is the use of the colloquial term understood to translate the English word tomorrow – "*bukra*". It is particularly frustrating to many Westerners living in Islamic countries when an expectation involving "*bukra*" is unfulfilled, or when a proposed deadline goes by without resolution – and without any apparent concern about the deadline. It is more helpful to understand

112 Here it would be helpful to translate *in sha Allah* as "unless God has other plans for me".

113 Gen 1:26-27.

114 See page 14 above.

that in Islam it is entirely presumptuous to express future events with any precision because the future is entirely in God's hands. "*Bukra*" more accurately refers to sometime soon, or sometime early, rather than the specific day which follows the current day. This is not an unwillingness to make a commitment or take responsibility, but rather a code of behaviour based on both piety and simple social tradition. An individual who insists on precision and commitment regarding future events can experience great frustration and disappointment. Worse, he/she could easily find that Muslim colleagues or friends distance themselves because they perceive their friend as having no self-respect or manners. Non-Muslims who insist on planning precisely, or express an expectation that a Muslim friend should acceed to a Western understanding of accountability for a future commitment are perceived by Muslims as arrogant in the least, even blasphemous at times. Humans cannot possibly know for sure what time something might happen on a future day; this degree of certainty can be attributed to God only!

Western post-enlightenment Christian culture has developed over the centuries based on an understanding that humanity is creative, and that because humans are made in the image and likeness of God we participate with God in creativity. Christian theology looks at creation as an ongoing process, evidenced in the Incarnation itself, with humanity in partnership with God as stewards of the creation.[115] Another way to express this concept would be to say that in Christianity and in Judaism humanity shares a management responsibility with God in stewardship of creation and the outworking of society and history. This belief is completely incompatible with Islam.[116] Conservative Muslims would classify this concept as *shirk*, attributing characteristics to a human that only rightfully belong to God.

---

115 Karl Rahner, *Encyclopedia of Theology, The Concise Sacramundum Mundi* (New York, The Seabury Press, 1975), 695-659.

116 "What God knows and does is eternal and necessary and can't be changed, and no individual will, no knowledge of singulars or contingency, is possible to God. He doesn't concern himself with things like us, and you can't talk about human beings as images of God… For Jews and Christians, human beings are made in the image of God. For Islam, to conceive of an image of God is to fall very short, even to falsify, His greatness. To speak of images of God is blasphemy. It marks one as an infidel – one who has not seen the point, and is in denial about the inconceivable greatness of God". Michael Novak, 'Another Islam', *First Things,* 127 (2002), 17.

Remember, *Shirk* is the foremost offence in Islam. Michael Novak, winner of the Templeton Prize and holder of the Fredreck Jewett Chair in Religious and Public Policy at the American Enterprise Institute suggests,

> Focusing on God's transcendence is Islam's great strength. Its weakness is that it can say little about human liberty, and about how human choice affects the will of God. How can God allow for human freedom? How can God permit human choice? It's as though medieval Muslims imagined liberty to be a zero-sum game. If humans have it, God doesn't. If God has it, humans don't. It's a philosophical problem they couldn't resolve.[117]

We must continue to remind ourselves that the word *Islam* means submission. Muslims are not so much concerned about moral choices but about conformity to guidelines, to 'follow the straight path' as presented in the *Qur'an* and *Hadith*.[118] Obedience and submission is more about right actions than about right morals.

The reader must understand that this is not a debate about free will and determinism as in classic Christian apologetics; it is, rather, a fundamental understanding of God's greatness and human dependence on God. In Islam God's mercy is a principal expression of his identity; of the ninety-nine names of God revered in Islam, *Al-Raheem* (The Merciful) is by far one of the most often invoked. Of course there are similar perspectives in Christian thinking, where submissiveness entails the work of discerning God's will and following it. In Christian thinking, knowing the will of God and deciding to act differently is one Christian definition of sin. But for the Muslim, even the claim to know the will of God is almost blasphemous. It presumes an intimacy with God that contradicts God's transcendence. Again – *Shirk!*

All of the above presumes thinking, deciding and acting on the level of the individual. That in itself is a particularly American approach to defining responsibility and morality. Muslims in America and Americans living in Islamic countries each often find themselves facing a steep learning curve in adapting to a lifestyle permeated with what seems like contradictory

---

117 Novak, 17.

118 Halstead, 284.

Cloth/material shop in the market in Taiz, Yemen

Street vendors in a street in Taiz, Yemen

value systems. Keeping in mind the importance of *Tawheed*, and that Islamic society stresses coherence and conformity rather than individuality and innovation, we can begin to see the difficulty for Muslims to initiate individual decisiveness or place importance on personal responsibility in the same way that Western culture presumes.

For Muslims it is not natural to approach morality issues from an individual perspective. "The concept of *ijma* (consensus) has always been and continues to be a dominant concept in the understanding of Islam, based on the Prophet's assurance that 'my community will not agree on error.' *Ijma* has been used to maintain a close correlation between Islam as revealed and the religious life as lived."[119] Muslims are much more comfortable making decisions as a group rather than as individuals. There is security in consensus, risk in individuality.[120] Perhaps this difference in approach can be understood helpfully by looking at the way the two cultures approach the concept of innovation.

> Originally intended to protect the young religion from premature reform and distortion, *bid'a* became a symbol of Muslim distrust of all kinds of innovations and inventions. While the word *innovation* has a positive connotations (sic) in the English language, the word *bid'a* in Islamic discourse carries negative and sinful implications. The concept of *bid'a* came to symbolize a fundamental Muslim resistance to change.[121]

Innovation, in Islam, is something of a contradiction to the purpose of revelation.[122] What has been revealed is immutable; change in general threatens the security of social conformity to the *Sunnah*. Western culture encourages initiative, a willingness to make mistakes, and to learn from

---

119 Haddad, 144.

120 Of course this is true in any cultural context. The difference here is the religious connection.

121 Ali A. Mazrui, 'Islam and the United States: streams of convergence, strands of divergence', *Third World Quarterly*, 25, 5 (2004), 813.

122 "A'isha reported *Allah's* Messenger as saying: He who innovates things in our affairs for which there is no valid reason commits sin and these are to be rejected. *...He who did any act for which there is no sanction from our behalf, that is to be rejected. Sahih Muslim vol 3, 931.*

Camels wandering onto the road, and blocking traffic, in rural Saudi Arabia

our mistakes. Risk-taking is seen as courageous and important in the quest for prosperity. Failure is not necessarily considered shameful in Western culture,[123] especially if one is perceived to have overcome failure. Even the *potential* of shame associated with failure or mistakes is a very serious matter in Islamic culture. Western culture places such a high value on innovation and risk-taking that Westerners experience a high degree of frustration when interacting, especially in the workplace, with a cultural value which holds innovation and creativity as suspect, or even a sinful, value. Coupled with the strong importance of decisions being made through consultation (*shura*), these dimensions of Islamic society do not interact well with a value system based on individual decision-making or personal initiative, particularly initiative that involves taking risks.

Muslims are commanded to make every effort to promote Islam, and to defend Islam. Because honour and loyalty are imperative social values, all Muslims are expected to participate in the process of strengthening the community, and working to ensure that anything which could threaten the

123 Bernard Lewis, *Cultures in Conflict* (Oxford: Oxford University Press, 1995), 75.

cohesiveness of society is disallowed.[124] "By the fifteenth century CE, the famous Muslim historian Ibn Khaldun was able to define the discipline of *kaläm* (theology) as 'a science that involves arguing with rational proofs in defence of articles of faith and refuting innovators who deviate in their dogmas from the doctrines of the early generations and the people of tradition.' The core of these dogmas is the oneness of God."[125] A modern manifestation of this way of thinking is the establishment of departments or committees in some Islamic countries for "The Promotion of Virtue and the Prevention of Vice." These committees are charged with matters like censorship of literature, movies and advertisements on a more formal scale, but also for implementing public standards like dress codes in shopping malls. Foreign products of all kinds, especially advertising and the entertainment industry, and lifestyle patterns of non-Muslims living in Islamic countries are all especially a matter of attention for these committees because any kind of foreign influence is a potential corruption to the **purity** of the Islamic society. For example, food additives may have pork extract or alcoholic content. Print media or retail packaging may be too graphic, or promote products/activities inconsistent with the preservation of the Islamic community standards. These guardians of the faith may be official in some countries, or self-appointed in others.

The combination of contrasts between individuality/identity and community/identity, the differing foci on God's imminent involvement/control in our daily affairs, and very differing values about right/wrong and shame/honour combine to form very subtly different value systems which guide everyday decisions, commitments, and even the sense of personal accountability. It deeply affects the values we place on specificity, precision and planning. Westerners living in an Islamic society can expect to encounter Muslims who express concern about behaviour, activities, commercial practices, or political policies which, in their minds, threaten to diminish the Islamic character of society. For example, the Iranian fixation on America as *The Great Satan* during the revolution in 1979 (and ever since among some

124 Wai-Yip Ho, 'Danish cartoon controversy in the Chinese context: transnational Islam and public visibility of Hong Kong Muslims', *Contemporary Islam*, 3, 3 (2009), 284.

125 Ahmed E. Souaiaia, 'Reasoned and inspired beliefs: a study of Islamic theology', *Muslim World*, 97, 2 (2007), 334.

Iranians) was based on a need to identify an *outside* source/influence of change that Muslims should reject. Modernity inevitably implies change, and change threatens the stability of the status quo. Movies, music, fashion and other influences from outside the Islamic community which entice Muslims to change their lifestyle are all a threat to the coherent Islamic identity of society.[126] Changes in the education system, workplace, family roles of both men and women, and political decisions based on secular values are all seen as un-Islamic imports from the non-Muslim world, America in particular. Many Muslims are concerned about losing their historic, cultural (Islamic) identity in the face of all of this change, which therefore should be resisted at ALL costs.

These differing definitions of responsibility, perceived as eminating from the individual or from the community produces very differing expressions of social identity. Western Christians have difficulty understanding Islamic values, partly because Islamic definitions of social interaction are based on concepts of 'clean and unclean', permitted and forbidden, rather than 'right and wrong.' These standards of behaviour apply to what Christians would consider spiritual dimensions and social interactions equally, because of course there is no secular/sacred dichotomy in Islam.

---

126 Halstead, 288.

7. UNCLEAN AND CLEAN (Haram & Halal)

***In* fiqh *(jurisprudence) all actions fall into one of five categories: prohibited (*haram*), discouraged (*makruh*), neutral (*mubah*), recommended (*mustahabb/mandub*), and obligatory (*fard*).*[127]**

Many Western Christians find social interaction among and between Muslims difficult to understand, and consequently some experience discomfort or even offence in the context of these unfamiliar experiences. Factors directing social protocols and habits which affect interaction between individuals are learned in childhood, through observation and imitation, and largely function on the subconscious level of the brain. When an individual encounters a system of social interaction based on protocols different from her/his own, it is often disorienting[128] and embarrassing mistakes are not unusual. Because Western culture promotes radical individuality and equality, cultural norms prohibiting certain forms of social interaction can be offensive, or at least confusing. A good understanding of the role of ritual purity in Islamic culture can alleviate many of these problems, and enhance the ability to engage in business and social relationships with confidence.

Most modern people are conscious of the concept of clean and unclean food. Many Hindus are, by religious conviction, vegans or vegetarians. Almost everyone knows that Jews and Muslims don't eat pork. Other foods, and methods of preparing foods, also figure strongly in what is allowed to be eaten and what is not allowed for both Muslims and Jews. For Christians there are few points of comparison to give an experiential understanding of the depth of meaning and pervasive influence of purity laws in non-Christian religions unless the individual has first-hand experience of a religious community that practices purity laws. "The modern mind finds it difficult to look sympathetically at the habit of mind which puts the ritual and the ethical on the same level of significance."[129]

For Christians, all things are 'clean'. (Mark 7:19b, Acts 11:2-30; Romans

---

127 Glasse 170.

128 Duane Elmer, *Cross-Cultural Conflict: Building Relationships for Effective Ministry* (Downers Grove, Ill.: Intervarsity Press, 1993), 17.

129 David Daiches, *Moses* (New York: Praeger Publishers, 1975), 141.

14:14a) Therefore, Christians don't normally encounter purity laws[130] except as they relate to the Old Testament scripture where various states of existence are described as unclean, requiring ritual washings and other ritual duties for reinstatement to religious *and* social acceptance:[131] leprosy (Leviticus 13:44), post-partum (Leviticus 12:2,5), menstruation (Leviticus 15:19), sexual intercourse (Leviticus 15:2), are but a few. We find in the Bible that contact with anyone or anything that is categorised as unclean contaminates oneself, and disqualifies the contaminated person from contact with God/Yahweh and, by extension, God's people. This natural extension of the concept of contamination means that the person who comes in contact with uncleanness in any way is therefore cut off from social interaction also, until ritual purity can be regained through the proscribed process.[132] Basically, the concept that the unclean contaminates the clean is consistent in many world religions, particularly Islam.

These considerations in the context of 'clean and unclean' have social and relational dimensions rarely considered any more in our secular society. Western Christians are not pre-disposed to comprehend the importance of ritual washings and food preparation requirements prevalent in Islamic societies, except in ways that can be related to health and hygiene. In spite of the 'contamination' imagery connected to ritual purity, the most important way for Christians to approach an understanding of ritual purity in Islam is not a comparison with health and hygiene, but rather to consider the transcendental nature of God, and the Biblical definition of holiness. Basically, the Biblical distinction between the clean and unclean was related to cult, for it was in terms of service to Yahweh, either in active worship or simply in being his covenanted people, that integrity was demanded. To be unclean was to lack holiness, and such was viewed not as a moral condition, but as a state of being, incompatible with the holiness of Yahweh and hence

130 A comment might be helpful here: that the revelation in the New Testament assures Christians that "all things are clean" is not the point of discussion. The intention here is to give the reader a basis for understanding Islamic culture and an opportunity for learning to interact with Muslims in an inoffensive manner.

131 Raymond Edward Brown,, Joseph A. Fitzmyer, and Roland E. Murphy, *The New Jerome Bible Commentary* (Bangalore: Theological Publications in India, 1991), 68-72.

132 Among others, see Lev 11, Lev 15 and Num 19 for various descriptions of states of uncleanness, and purifying requirements.

prohibitive of any contact with him.[133]

In the thoughts of many, Christians and Muslims alike, religion is all about making ourselves acceptable to a transcendent God who is wholly 'other', unapproachable. Orthodox Christian theology tells us that God, in spite of our sinfulness, approaches us in Christ.[134] In other words, because we cannot make ourselves acceptable to God he accomplishes that for us through atonement[135] and adoption. Because Muslims understand God to be merciful but somewhat capricious and unknowable, Muslims possess a very strong awareness of the many aspects of life that give rise to impurity and imperil the possibility of obtaining God's mercy.[136]

The impetus to maintain or regain ritual purity drives many social customs and expectations in Islamic cultures. Purification is a high aspiration for all practicing Muslims. As *Surah* 2 states: *"For God loves those who turn to him constantly and he loves those who keep themselves pure and clean"* (2:222). Similar to Jewish codification of purity laws of the Old Testament, over the centuries Islamic scholars have codified all aspects of human life and have compiled a large collection of ablutions and preparatory prayers and recommendations for ensuring acceptability in performing religious rites. At the same time, Arab Islamic culture has evolved to accommodate the positives and negatives of life, balancing ritual with other daily routines. Books offering advice on how to be a good Muslim will always have a significant section devoted to the proper method of ablution for various

---

133 Brown, 68.

134 Rom 5:6-8 God, knowing that our sinfulness is a barrier between us and him, overcomes the barrier in coming to us in our sinfulness and sanctifies us in the life, death, resurrection and ascension of Jesus.

135 George Arthur Buttrich, ed., *The Interpreter's Dictionary of the Bible 1: A-D* (Nashville: Abingdon Press, 1962), 309-313.

136 *Sahih Muslim* 0435/0444/0447.This concept is expressed throughout popular Arabic literature and novels. Consider the following reference in a popular novel by Naguib Mafhouz, for example: "He was hesitant about going to the mosque, for he lacked the courage to proceed directly there following his pursuit of a woman during the time set aside for prayer. Had not his frolic terminated the requisite state of ritual cleanliness? Did it not render him unfit to stand before his Compassionate Lord? In pain he sadly gave up the idea of going to prayers and walked the streets aimlessly for about an hour. Then he returned home, reflecting once more on his sin." Naguib Mahfouz, *Palace of Desire* (Reading, Berks.: Black Swan, 1994), 97.

aspects of daily life.[137]

Many Christians know that Muslims are required to pray five times each day. What they don't often recognise is that there are particularly prescriptive ablutions that should be performed before prayer. Christians who interact with Muslims find that Muslims have difficulty understanding the Christian assumption that a person can pray or worship without ritual washing. In Islam, incomplete or out of sequence washing can invalidate the ablution and so invalidates prayer itself. Devout Muslims are very conscientious about strict adherence to the protocols of ablution. Therefore public toilets in shopping malls and airports in Islamic countries have architectural features designed to facilitate the required ablutions for daily prayer. Mosques are either located next to a public washing area or have an ablutions area built in. Conversely, public toilet areas that *don't* have ablution facilities are often awash with splashed water at prayer times because of the difficulty of washing feet in normal sinks at counter height!

These points are of course obvious to the casual observer. There are multitude habits and customs relating to ritual purity that are not so obvious.[138] Many social customs are expressed in ways that increase the likelihood of ensuring ritual purity. It is unusual for Muslims to touch another person with the left hand, to touch or to offer food with the left hand,[139] because the left hand is the "toilet hand" used for personal hygiene. Shoes are not worn in mosques. Wardrobes for both men and women are supposed to be very modest, to guard against impure thoughts which would therefore require a repetition of ritual washing.[140]

Anything that is holy must remain unsullied in the way it is used, even for religious purposes. Among Muslims it is disrespectful to set a copy of the *Qur'an* on the floor, or to place anything over or on top of a *Qur'an* that is sitting on a table or shelf. Conversely, Muslims are astonished when a Christian might treat a Bible with any less respect than a Muslim treats

---

137 One such example: Abu Bakr Jabir Al-Jaza'iry, *Minhaj Al-Muslim* (Riyadh: Darussalam, 2001), 372-79. Mubarak Ali, 12-22.

138 For example: Shad, 78-80.

139 Shad, 8. See also, *Sahih Muslim* 5007/5008/5010/5012.

140 See Mubarak Ali, 23-24; Shad, 88.

a *Qur'an*. Muslims know that Christians consider the Bible to be a holy book, and they cannot understand how a Christian would defile a holy book with underlining or highlighting. Toilet areas are unclean. Therefore, it is "disliked"[141] to wear jewellery with the name of Allah inscribed in the toilet, or much worse, to read the *Qur'an* while in the bathroom or even have a newspaper which might have a *Qur'anic* verse printed.[142] Muslim visitors in Christian homes find it very strange to see a Bible verse hung on the wall of a bathroom!

As a point of clarity, as well as matters of ritual purity, the *Sunnah* of Islam defines what is forbidden (*haram*) or what is lawful (*halal*) – something rather different than the emphasis on clean or unclean. Pork and alcohol, for example, are forbidden – not unclean. If a Muslim finds he has inadvertently eaten pork or a product with a pork ingredient in it he has become unclean and must perform the required ablution before being restored to prayer or participation in society. In this context, the manifestation of the problem is not so much a question of sin or purity, but of influences that pollute Muslims or Islamic society. Much daily interaction in Islamic countries, as well as interaction between Muslims and Christians in the workplace or in restaurants in the USA is hugely influenced by this principle.

This is very important, because it reflects the Islamic value of the *Ummah*, the corporate identity of Islam. Purity and pollution are not only personal, but communal. The customs departments in many Islamic countries restrict the importation of goods which, among other things, contain pork derivatives[143] or alcohol content[144] or publications which could even remotely be construed as sexually titillating.[145] These restrictions are very pervasive, and non-Muslims living in Islamic countries often find that their personal habits around food preparation, social interaction, and the pursuit

141 "Disliked" is a literal translation of the Arabic word describing this practice.

142 Shalhub, Fuad ibn Abd al-Az iz, *The Book of Manners* 1st ed. (Riyadh; Houston; Darussalam, 2003), 232.

143 *I.e.*, various food products, pork bristle hair brushes, even references to pigs in school textbooks.

144 *I.e.*, some mouthwashes, vanilla extract, barbecue sauces.

145 This would include outright pornography, fashion magazines, books, and particular styles of advertising.

of personal hobbies require significant adjustment!

The attention given to Halal and Haram aspects of life, both on the personal and the social levels, is an indicator of how deeply religious values determine the smallest factors that direct the ways in which Islamic societies function. We will move on to explore the relationship between religion and society more specifically and in broader terms in the next chapter.

8. RELIGION AND SOCIETY

To the modern mind, culture is the most encompassing concept of man's intellectual and social activities. To the mind of the orthodox Muslim, religion is still more encompassing. Culture is concerned with what is here, but religion is concerned with what is here and in the hereafter. In modern as well as medieval Islam, the distinction between religion and culture, as well as the distinction between traditional and rational science, took place under the impact of foreign cultures and sciences. There is no ground for such a distinction in the Koran.[146]

Any attempt to understand Islamic society, and particularly Arab Islam, cannot be divorced from the *Qur'anic* emphasis on the fundamental oneness of God.[147] In earlier chapters, we explored how the Islamic concept of *Tawheed* establishes a corporate and social responsibility to Allah, while Christian tradition emphasises a personal response to God. Inevitably, these very different understandings of God's interaction with humanity will be expressed in very differing cultural patterns. The breadth, depth and intensity of the concept of unity in Arab/Islamic society may be especially difficult for a person with a secular/Western mind-set to comprehend.

The *Ummah* (brotherhood of all Muslims; the social expression of *Tawheed*) incorporates a vision for unity that transcends national, ethnic, linguistic and historic loyalties. One way to describe the *Ummah* would be to use the word 'family' in many concentric references: nuclear, extended, tribal, ethnic/religious, national. The secular mindset is focused upon the individual and does not begin to comprehend the degree of mutuality of identity and unity that defines Islamic social and familial interrelationships. In addition, in recent history there is an increasing polarisation within Islamic society stemming from conflicting understandings of the *Ummah* in response to modern political and social ideas imported from other cultures and influencing Islamic societies. To begin with, a short overview of the role of Muhammad as 'leader of the people' and the development of the

---

146 Saab, 149.

147 Saab, 147. In Islam, the sacred is the wholly other, the One and Unique God, Allah. Islam is in a sense a passionate protest against attribution of sacredness to anyone or anything but Allah.

historic Caliphate could be helpful.

*Surely those who swear allegiance to you do but swear allegiance to Allah; the hand of Allah is above their hands. Therefore whoever breaks (his faith), he breaks it only to the injury of his own soul, and whoever fulfills what he has covenanted with Allah, He will grant him a mighty reward (*Surah 48:10*).*

*Whoever obeys the Apostle, he indeed obeys Allah, and whoever turns back, so We have not sent you as a keeper over them (*Surah 4:80*).*

These verses from the *Qur'an*[148] can give some sense of the Muslim's understanding of Muhammad's position in Islamic society. Swearing allegiance to the Prophet Muhammad and obeying the revelation of God are inseparably linked. Obedience to Muhammad *is* obedience to God.[149] Muslims understand that God appointed Muhammad not only as a prophet who revealed God's message, but also as the viceroy of God to lead God's society in right behaviour and values by both proclamation and personal example.[150] Understanding this emphasis on emulating the personal habits and lifestyle manifestations of the person/Prophet Muhammad should help us understand why Muslims instinctively think that Jesus is to Christians what Muhammad is to Muslims. When Christians allow or use that comparison we diminish the incarnate reality of Christ. The admonition to 'be Christ-like' has much more to do with daily living into our inheritance of the resurrection life than a struggle to maintain particular behavioural

---

148 See also 59:7b, 33:6, 4:13-14, 4:59, 3:132. Further references are abundant. One only needs to run a search of the word "obey" in the *Qur'an* to find how many verses link obedience to the Prophet as obedience to God's revelation.

149 *Surah* 4:80 He who obeys the Apostle, obeys God: But if any turn away we have not sent thee to watch over their (evil deeds).

150 Yusuf Ali's commentary on *Surah* 4:80 says, "The Apostle was sent to preach, guide, instruct, and show the Way, – not to drive people to good, or to detect all that was evil. That is not God's Plan, which trains the human Will. The Apostle's duty is therefore to convey the Message of God, in all the ways of persuasion that are open to him. If men perversely disobey that Message, they are not disobeying him but they are disobeying God. In the same way those who obey the Message are obeying God. They are not obliging the Messenger. They are merely doing their duty." Abdullah Yusuf Ali, *An English Interpretation of the Holy Qur-an with Full Arabic Text*. (Lahore: Sh. Mu-hammad Ashraf, 1975), 204.

patterns. Muslims' imitation of the Prophet Muhammad is the basis of behavioural values in Islamic families and societies.

Muslims believe that in Muhammad God restored the role of the Caliph, which Muslims understand to have been in abeyance since Adam, and that successive Muslim Caliphs over the centuries have personally embodied the life of the Islamic community. In the words of Glasse, "The Prophet was at once patriarch, revealer, priest, and prince; and thus over the years the Caliph has been called his "shadow in history… The idea of the Caliphate is, however, that of a sacred function and not merely a public office."[151] Modern Islam is still deeply influenced by the writings of Ibn Taimiyyah[152] (1263-1328CE), who held that the political ruler is a religious ruler, and is responsible before God. Therefore his rule is granted by God and not the people.[153]

For the many Muslims who ascribe to the pursuit of a "pure" form of Islam, the ruler holds a sacred trust. He is responsible to guide his people and preserve them from all threats. That responsibility includes not only the threat of war or poverty, but also moral corruption and non-Islamic influences. Another way to present this responsibility would be to say that the ruler is accountable before God *and* his people to preserve the Islamic character of the society against all influences. There can be no unity if there is deviance. Conformity is essential. Independent action, or personal initiative that sets an individual apart, is not highly valued, and usually discouraged, within the community.

From the *Hijra*[154] until the beginning of the 20th century the whole of Islamic society was basically perceived as a monolithic culture led by a single caliph, although the Ottomans, because they were not Arab, substituted the

---

151 Glassé, p100.

152 It would not be incorrect to compare Ibn Taimiyyah's influence in Islam to that of Aquinas or Augustine in Christian tradition.

153 Rolf Hille, 'Human rights and Islam – is the 'clash of civilizations' already pre-programmed?', *Evangelical Review of Theology*, 30 (2006), 356.

154 This denotes Muhammad's departure from Mecca to Medina in 622 prompted by the opposition of the merchants of Mecca and marking the consolidation of the first Muslim community.

term "sultan" instead of caliph.[155] Throughout Islamic history, the process of absorbing many different cultures in creating the Islamic empire did incorporate considerable diversity, but there was never any disagreement with the principle that the Caliph, as the successor of Muhammad, embodied God's will for the people of Islam in exercising central authority. Of course, there were times in Islamic history when the Caliph's embodiment of God's leadership of the people was more ceremonial than real, with others exercising 'power behind the throne', but this emphasises even more how important the person of the Caliph has been, historically, in Islamic society. How the leader/Caliph was selected eventuated in the main divisions of Islam, Shia/Sunni in particular, but the principle of unitary leadership was always and continues to be affirmed and sought after in Islamic society. *Surah* 4:59 says: *'Obey God, and obey the Apostle and those charged with authority among you'*; while *Surah* 3 states:

> *O you who believe! Observe your duty to God with right observance, and die not save as those who have surrendered; and hold fast, all of you together, to the 'guidance' of God, and do not separate. Then there may spring from you a nation who invite to goodness, and enjoin right conduct and forbid indecency. (*Surah 3:102-105*).*

Islam looks for social coherence, right relationships between human beings, maintained through mutual submission to God's revealed law (Shari'a/Sunnah).[156] In order for a Western mind to understand this concept it is essential to comprehend the profound *mutuality* of this submission among Muslims, creating a human social unity (*Ummah*) that reflects the oneness of God himself. Certainly, Christian teaching would emphasise that each individual's participation in the salvation offered in Christ should be manifest by daily submission to, and participation in, the purpose of God. And to the degree in which a greater percentage of persons in society would do so, Christians understand that society would more and more

155 The Arabic word *sultan (Al Mawrid: 640)* indicates 'power/authority", while the Arabic word caliph *(Glassé: 100; Al Mawrid: 521)* denotes the concept of descendant/successor.

156 "Islam is not just a religion, and certainly not just a fundamentalist political movement. It is a civilization, and a way of life that varies from one Muslim country to another but is animated by a common spirit far more humane than most Westerners realize." Mazrui, 'Islamic and Western Values', *Foreign Affairs*, 76, 5 (1997), 118.

reflect God's intention for society. And here is where we find the precise sociological distinction between Christianity, particularly as we encounter it among evangelically-minded Christians, and Islam as experienced in Arab Culture. In Christian thinking, individuals make society; society is made up of individuals. Islam, on the other hand, calls for the whole of society to be submitted to God, and the individual to be conformed to this social norm; individuality emanates from society. Therefore, in Islam, the individual does not define society; society defines the individual. It is a subtle but enormous difference in the perception of the function of society, the individual's social identity, and the role of religion in defining that relationship.

People nurtured in a secular society and imbued with secular values are ill equipped to understand the relationship between religion and society as it is found in countries where Islam is the dominant social character. In the words of David Little, "…social scientists, policy makers, and human rights specialists have failed until recently to appreciate the political and international significance of religion because of an overzealous and undiscriminating belief in the inevitability of secularisation. What has now become obvious is that far from eliminating religious passion, secular pressures often intensify it."[157]

While most Westerners would acknowledge an important role for religion among the many values that define society, modern secular society positively enshrines individual choices and personal freedoms. Christianity indeed emphasises the need for believers to make personal choices that reflect the person's saving relationship in Christ; the Christian heritage also assumes that many people will choose to deny Christ, and choose to go against the Christian "flow". Secular society as it is experienced in the USA insists, along with most intentional Christians in America, that freedom to choose to either follow or reject God's revelation is a paramount value. Therefore, religious adherence, practice or belief is seen to be a personal matter, and a personal choice. However, the opportunity to choose, to go against the dictates of society which is by definition a reflection of God's Law is, in itself, abhorred in Islam. The essence of *Ummah* is derived from conformity to the *Sunnah*; it is enacted in conformity to society. The idea

---

157 David Little, Rethinking human rights: a review essay on religion, relativism, and other matters', *Journal of Religious Ethics*, 27, 1 (1999), 155.

of encouraging a private individual to reject his/her role in society is almost unthinkable.[158] Some of us are old enough to remember the ostracised draft dodgers who fled to Canada during the Vietnam War, and how difficult it was for them to return after the war was over. Apostasy in Islam is SO much more radically unthinkable precisely because it is much more than a choice to follow a different religious system. It is seen as a rejection of sacred family, social and cultural values.

A case in point: American society applies a specific definition to the kind of criminals who engage in violent acts designed to undermine American influence and policies, calling them terrorists. It is understood that society needs protection from these criminals, like other criminals, by isolating them from society in prisons, and that the threat/risk of incarceration should provide a deterrent against additional similar criminal activity. The society of Saudi Arabia refers to these people as "deviants" rather than criminals.[159] The underlying assumption involved is that a) the individual has misunderstood and deviated from the true path of Islam; and b) the person can be reformed and society healed by bringing him back into conformity with the accepted definition of Islamic norms.[160] Saudi culture understands the long-term solution to this kind of deviation to entail a more thorough integration in society rather than separation through incarceration. One way to express this subtle conceptual difference is to say that one culture sees the terrorist as a person who is acting to destroy society and the other sees the terrorist as a person whose actions corrupt society.

Increasingly, religious Muslims reject secularisation as corrupt and "synthetic"[161] precisely because it has moved away from specifically

---

158 Here we should briefly reflect on the perception of apostasy/conversion from Islam to another religion as a social evil rather than a theological conviction. The topic deserves a chapter on its own.

159 "The Saudi programme views terrorists as confused and angry young men. It treats their extremism as a social disease bred by poverty, lack of education and xenophobia." Fisher, Max. 2009. 'Applying Saudi Counterterrorism to the Afghanistan War', *The Atlantic (online)*, (2009), 1.

160 Christopher Boucer, 'Saudi Arabia's "Soft" Counterterrorism Strategy: Prevention, Rehabilitation, and Aftercare', *Carnegie Endowment for International Peace*, 97 (2008), 15.

161 Judith Miller, God Has *Ninety-Nine Names: Reporting from a Militant Middle East* (New York: Simon & Schuster, 1996): 60, 95.

religious definitions of social values. Secularism, with its emphasis on individuality in private belief, is seen to negate the role of religion in society. The idea that a person can hold religious beliefs that are not publicly manifest is counter-intuitive to Muslims; it is simply not a religious belief if it is strictly personal.[162] And to reflect more strongly on secular values in American society, it would not be incorrect to say that it is inconceivable in Islam to be a "non-religious" person. As Sayyid Qutb, the hugely influential writer (and some would say the ideologue of Al Qa'eda) wrote in 1949,

> For as the popular saying goes, 'Religion concerns only a man and his God.' How have we arrived at *this* strange view...? We have imported it... for certainly the fable of a divorce between faith and life did not grow up in the Muslim East, nor does Islam know of it...[163]

Furthermore, it is very difficult for Muslims to comprehend a religious identity primarily based on "right belief" because Islam is about a "way of life". "The proper response of Muslims is not so much believing *in* the faith but responding *to* the faith. Islam, in this sense, is not so much a noun but a verb, an action."[164] Muslims submit to God in their submission to society; society is perceived as the reflection of God's will on earth. Belonging is essential, and belonging takes on many different characteristics. B.A. Roberson, in the introduction to her compendium discussing Current Islamic Reformation states that,

> "...the assertion of a Muslim community is intimately related to the strength of shared norms, that is, *Ummah* entails not only a common Muslim community facing other non-Muslim peoples, but is dependent upon the espousal by that community of its internal values and faith, and fulfillment of duty."[165]

The development of Arab nationalism after the collapse of the Ottoman

---

162 The idea of a convert living in Islamic society as a 'secret believer' in Christ is only comprehensible as far as fear for one's life can cause a person to sublimate his identity. People nurtured in Islamic society cannot easily envisage such a contradictory existence.

163 Qutb, 20.

164 Ball, 317.

165 B. A. Roberson, *Shaping the Current Islamic Reformation* (London: Frank Cass, 2003): 25.

Empire (creating independent Arab countries of Jordan, Iraq, Syria, Lebanon, Egypt, etc.) conflicted in many ways with the concept of the caliphate, the one-ness of society and the one-ness of God.[166] Should one's identity be as an Egyptian Muslim or a Muslim Egyptian? An Arab Palestinian Muslim, or a Muslim Palestinian Arab? Or simply an Arab Muslim?[167] And, while this dilemma was and still is very, very real, a paradox exists in that the layers of identity are often so blurred that there is little perceived perplexity. The more conservative the Islamic individual or family, the less the dilemma was felt, essentially because *all* of the identities were absorbed in the *Ummah*. Increasingly in the past 30 years, influences attempting to reassert the importance of the caliphate and the transnational *Ummah* are dominating political and social debate in the modern Islamic world, calling for a common Islamic identity which supersedes nationality and even language. This trend became readily apparent in the aftermath of the Iraqi invasion of Kuwait in August of 1990. The image of Muslim *nations* at war with each other shocked Muslims the world over, and for many, discredited Arab nationalism irreparably.

In recent years increasing polarisation has surfaced within Islam as Islamic thinkers and politicians wrestle with this dilemma. Muslims disagree vehemently about the nature of the *Ummah*. Like many conservative Christians who are disillusioned with post-modern social trends, many conservative Muslims are looking back to a "golden age" of Islam under the caliphate when all Muslims were ruled under a single government. This trend rejects nationalisms which, in their view, compartmentalise Islam by secularly defined sub-identities. To make matters worse, modern national boundaries are deemed to have been imposed by Western "colonial" powers in the aftermath of WWI and quite often do not reflect either Arab or Islamic historical identities. For over a generation, this debate and disillusionment within Islam has been gaining strength, and unfortunately more and more violent expression, based on the conviction that the mutuality of Islamic social identity can no longer be found in a political expression but only in

166 Haddad, 149.

167 Where this dilemma leaves Arabic-speaking Christians is the very important subject of many other scholarly writings. One of the best treatments of this topic is *The Arab Christian* by Bishop Kenneth Cragg, *The Arab Christian: A History in the Middle East,* 1st ed. (Louisville, Ky.: Westminster/John Knox Press, 1991).

allegiance to *Shari'a* or divine law.[168] As a case in point, this is the rationale which supports the popularity of migrant *mujahideen*, people willing to give their lives in a struggle (*jihad*) to defend Islam in a location other than their home country from non-Islamic political or social influences.[169]

> *You shall not find a people who believe in Allah and the latter day befriending those who act in opposition to Allah and His Apostle, even though they were their (own) fathers, or their sons, or their brothers, or their kinsfolk; these are they into whose hearts He has impressed faith, and whom He has strengthened with an inspiration from Him: and He will cause them to enter gardens beneath which rivers flow, abiding therein; Allah is well-pleased with them and they are well-pleased with Him these are Allah's party: now surely the party of Allah are the successful ones – (*Surah 58:22 *[underlining mine])*

It should be readily apparent that the individuality enshrined in secular culture presents a critical contrast between Western/secular and Islamic/religious definitions of society. Furthermore, it should be no surprise that republican democracy, as defined in the United States and encouraged by US foreign policy, is considered incompatible with true Islam by a great many Muslims. Part of the problem comes from the many differing uses of the word "democracy" in public statements. To many in the world it simply means an electoral process leading to the selection of national leadership. To others it can mean: protection/rights of minorities, free market economy, equal opportunity employment, or simply "the majority rules". Even a cursory consideration of these definitions of democracy will reveal that all of these values do not complement each other seamlessly. For example, Syria and Turkey have been internationally considered to be democratic

---

168 Sigvard Von Sicard, "Contemporary Islam and its world mission," *Missiology* 4, no. 3:341 (1976), 343.

169 Many people are familiar with the 'freedom fighters' who migrated to Afghanistan (supported by the US) to oppose the Soviets during the 80's. This model was repeated after the collapse of Yugoslavia when Muslims from the world around went to Bosnia to assist in the fighting against the Serbs. Many Muslims went to Iraq to help 'eject the foreign armies' after the fall of Saddam. Most recently, Muslims from many nations have joined the 'rebels' in Syria in the interest of eliminating a secularist government, (Assad's Baathist party) hoping to pave the way for an Islamic government in Syria.

governments, while human rights advocates would point out that "freedom of speech" is not facilitated in either of these two countries. Furthermore, depending on which democratic values are being analysed, criticism can be levied if imposition of democratically elected government does not protect minorities, as could be true in both of these countries.

Returning to the paradox that in America people define society, while in Islam society defines the people, it is useful to investigate how democracy is perceived in conservative Islam.

> Therefore, the typically democratic control of political power never takes place and the principle of the separation of powers also does not exist. Instead, Islamic fundamentalists base their government on the system of the *shura* according to *surah* 37, which says: 'And they perform their duties by mutual consent.' This concept of mutual consent or advice is declared by orthodox Muslims to be the real form of democracy without having to consider the modern legal structures of democracy.[170]

Typically, important decisions in Islamic societies are made by consensus of the parties involved. Consistent with the concept of the *Ummah*, the family, clan, tribe or nation traditionally arrives at important decision through a process of consultation among elders or responsible people. In traditional Islamic societies which encompass a large area this is referred to as a *shura*[171] council. These councils are often compared (mistakenly) to a parliamentary/congressional body. The fact that they are representative decision-making bodies is probably the only correct comparison. The same principle of consultative decision-making functions within regional identities, tribes, clans and the local extended family.

Participation on a *shura* council is not based on an election. The person participates because he, or in rare cases she, commands the respect of those who depend on him to look after their interests in the decision-making process. At the same time, the *shura* council members also command the respect of each other. They may not like each other and may even be enemies in armed conflict, but decisions cannot carry authority without the

170 Hille, 356.

171 The principle of consultative decision-making in Islamic societies.

participation of all involved and the consensus of the participants. There is no majority decision, but continued discussions until everyone agrees enough to present a unified way forward.[172] The process always takes time, but the end result ensures that every grouping within the *Ummah* comes out of the process with a sense of having a stake in the decision – and the idea is that there are no losers in the process.[173] Most Muslims would defend the conviction that a *shura* council is much more democratic than the American congressional system because it is inherently uniting whereas the American political system is seen as always inherently divisive.

To end this chapter, it would be good to reaffirm that the ideal goal of Islamic society is about harmony, and to a large degree, conformity. Society is seen to be an expression of mutuality borne out of common submission to the guidance God has given in the *Qur'an* and modeled in the life of The Prophet.[174] The ideal Islamic society's unity, very different from uniformity, is a reflection of the one-ness of God *because* God is the author of right social relationships. This runs counter to Western views of the rights and protection of individual belief. Moreso, it raises many questions about the rights and privileges extended to the individual in society. The next chapter will offer perspective about differing definitions regarding Human Rights and will shed yet further light on this paradox.

---

172 Here it is essential to remember that the concept of *unity* presumes diversity and should never be confused with the concept of *uniformity*.

173 Cate, 364.

174 Ezzati, 42.

9. HUMAN RIGHTS and RELIGIOUS FREEDOM

Before I discuss the human rights in Islam I would like to explain a few points about two major approaches to the question of human rights: the Western and Islamic. This will enable us to study the issue in its proper perspective and avoid some of the confusion which normally befogs such a discussion.[175]

The comment above, from a Muslim scholar generally understood to represent broadly conservative Islamic thinking, understates the dilemma human rights activists face in applying the Universal Declaration of Human Rights universally.[176] Christians the world over constantly impose their understanding of Human Rights in discussion with and about Muslims. Americans, in particular, often make the mistake of presuming that American values are superior to values of other cultures – or, worse, that American values ARE universal values. Although many people the world over do aspire to adopting various degrees of democracy, freedom and personal prosperity, it is a grave mistake to assume that all people in every part of the world share these values, *or that* it should be accepted that *all* people share them, *or that* they define these values in the same way. Indeed, what we have come to regard as 'American' values are regarded with suspicion and distrust by millions; the proclamation of the Universal Islamic Declaration of Human Rights as just one indicator. Exploring differing objections to the Universal Declaration of Human Rights will help bring understanding to Western difficulties in absorbing Muslims into Western culture, as well as difficulties Westerners experience when living in Islamic cultures.

Many, not only Islamic, cultures[177] in the modern world decry the secular

---

175 Syed abul Ala Maudoodi, *Human Rights in Islam* (Leicester: Islamic Foundation 1976). Preamble to chapter one.

176 It should be noted that this declaration was promulgated in 1948. Most Islamic countries which were members of the UN at that time were in some one or another way still associated with a colonial authority. Since then Afghanistan, Egypt, Syria, all of the Gulf states, Sudan, Libya, Indonesia, Pakistan, and other Islamic states all re-defined their identity (as more specifically Islamic) and their relationship to the UN between 1948 and 1980. Throughout this chapter I will refer to this document as the *Universal Declaration*.

177 Little, 153.

Western foundations upon which the original *Universal Declaration* was drafted. Islam in particular has engaged in thorough discussions, study and interpretation of human rights principles in relation to Islamic tradition and culture, under the authority of the *Sunnah*, and has been vocal in describing why the *Universal Declaration* cannot be held to be universal. "Iran... had taken an even stronger position, claiming that the Universal Declaration represents a secular outlook that cannot be implemented by Muslims and does not accord with the values recognised by Iran."[178]

Accordingly, an alternative *Universal **Islamic** Declaration of Human Rights* was proclaimed in Paris in 1981[179] to reflect opinion among a great many Muslim scholars on Human Rights as determined in the *Sunnah*, and also reflecting that the *Universal Declaration of Human Rights* adopted by the United Nations General Assembly on December 10, 1948 was based on a secular interpretation of the Judeo-Christian tradition.

> "What makes it so difficult for Muslims to recognise and to practise universal human rights? First of all the Islamic world understands itself as the *khair umma* (Surah 3, 110), that is, as the best society on earth. From this standpoint, there are great inner barriers to recognising the cultural achievements of non-Muslims and to learning from them... all non-Muslim influenced civilisations are devalued as *djahiliyya*, that is, as 'the age of ignorance without knowledge of the revelation of God to Mumammed'."[180]

In the view of a great many Muslims the UN declaration imposes values and expectations contrary to the Islamic *Sunnah*, and therefore should not be binding on Muslims or Islamic countries. Muslims are keen to proclaim that the *Sunnah* provides a basis of society with particular rights for all members, in keeping with the revealed will of God for the proper function of society. Also, among very conservative Muslims, Human Rights are

178 Little, 154.

179 The declaration is widely available on many websites and Islamic publications. I have chosen to use the version available on www.alhewar.com/islamdecl.html [accessed April 8, 2013] which includes annotations detailing further and more recent definition added by increasingly popular Islamic groups concerned with promoting a universal *ummah* based on *shari'a* rather than national identities. The entire text is included in Appendix 2 to this paper.

180 Hille, 355-6.

mandated from God for Muslims – not for non-Muslims.[181]

The conflict of interest here is most clearly represented in pointing out that the secularist foundation of the *Universal Declaration* presupposes that *society* has discovered and defines what is right and wrong, while the Islamic Declaration attempts to define rights in consistent interpretation of the *Sunnah*, being derived from *God himself*.

> "Rights in the sense of a legitimate expectation based on the moral duties of others seem to be in harmony with Islamic teaching, and indeed the term is used in this sense in the *Qur'an* and the *Hadith*. On the other hand, Islam is first and foremost the religion of submission (the literal meaning of *islam* is 'submission'), and the slave-master relationship is an important symbol of the believer's relationship with God. Rights, in the sense of self-assertion, 'I've got a right to do x' or in the sense of pressing a claim against God, or against a fellow human being, thus seem to run counter to the spirit of Islam."[182]

Because we have investigated the conflict with secularism in Islamic thought in other chapters we will restrict discussion in this chapter to some specific issues that plague the discussions between Islamic and Western applications of the concept of Human Rights. Westerners, even those who are deeply religious, approach the concept of human rights from a secular, non-religious point of view. This approach does not disregard the Judeo-Christian heritage that shines through the values presented in the *Universal Declaration*,[183] but it must also be acknowledged that those same Western Judeo-Christian values have also produced the value system that is now broadly expressed as secularism. Aside from the absolutely fundamental divide between a secular and a religious definition of society, examining some specific and somewhat popularly debated areas of divergence between Western and Islamic societies can bring insight to how and why the two different cultures define human rights differently. To cite a few examples: the difference in role and status of women in Western and Islamic societies

---

181 Hille, 358.

182 Halstead, 289.

183 I.e, Article One: They are endowed with reason and conscience and should act towards one another in a spirit of brotherhood. (Gal 5:14, Jam 2:8) See also Article 16.3, Article 25.2 (Dut 27:19 Ps 146:9), and others.

is mutually misunderstood and criticised by both cultures. Also, differing understandings of the role of minority (religious) groups in society and the concept of religious freedom hold little common ground for discussion.

Freedom of Religion

There is little ambiguity about what is meant by Freedom of Religion in a secular society. In America, by law, every individual must be afforded the opportunity to practice religious faith in accordance with his/her *personal* choice, and conversely, may not insist that another person follow the same religious ideals. The concept also embraces the principle that a person may, by choice, change religious identity and practice.[184] In Islam, Freedom of Religion is most often defined as the right for all Muslims to practice their faith within their own particular Islamic tradition (Shi'a, Sunni, or recognised subsets of each of these traditions.) The idea that a Muslim should be allowed to choose to NOT be a Muslim is incompatible with Islamic teaching. "[W]hen Islamic apologists quote the *Qur'anic* verse surah 2,256: 'no compulsion in religion', this has nothing to do with the free choice of religious affiliation. This context simply deals with a limited right to discuss the source texts of Sunni Islam, namely, the Qur'an and the Hadith, that is, the legal tradition of the words and deeds of the prophet, in a prescribed format."[185]

Islam presupposes that God is merciful to any human who practices justice and who believes in certain core tenets proclaimed in Islam; Monotheism, Angels, Judgment, etc. The *Qur'an* enjoins Muslims to not fight against non-believers who seek peace with the *Ummah*. At the same time, Muslims perceive themselves as a people appointed by God (3:110) to strive toward the establishment of Islamic society throughout the world.[186] The *Qur'an* also promises the faithful that they will be opposed by others on the basis of religion and in such cases the faithful are enjoined to fight against this opposition (9:73, 22:25, 22:39 and others). Among non-Muslims these verses seem to represent a built-in paradox for Muslims in their dealings

---

184 Ref. article 18 of the *Universal Declaration*.

185 Hille, 356.

186 Ansari, 443. See also *Qur'an* 3:104, 110, 114; 9:71 and 112.

with non-Muslims.

It is quite popular, and fundamentally flawed, to discuss freedom of religion in respect to Islam in the context of reciprocity. The absence of church buildings in Saudi Arabia, for instance, is compared to the fact that mosques exist in (almost) all 'Christian' countries. In fact, reciprocity is an incongruous context for discussion precisely because it is based on a secular, Western understanding of society. The fact that most Islamic countries have laws forbidding proselytising[187] is lamented by many who cite the complete freedom of Muslims to proselytise in democratic/secular countries of the world, and the perceived coercive pressures on Christians in Islamic countries to convert to Islam. For Muslims who believe that God has ordained that all humanity should embrace Islam, it is inconceivable that Islamic society should allow Muslims to become a non-Muslim. For some particularly conservative Muslims, even the presence of non-Muslims within the *Ummah* signifies something akin to corruption of the community, and the presence of buildings designated for non-Muslim religious ceremonies is perceived as a pollution of society. For instance, it is relatively common knowledge that churches are not allowed in Saudi Arabia, but few people know that non-Muslim burial is disallowed.[188] Reciprocation, as a concept, implies shared criteria on which to base what is exactly reciprocal. The differences between Islamic and Christian paradigms are serious enough to undermine any meaningful discussion based on reciprocation.

Democracy

In the discussion about human rights, the use of the term "democracy" has become a grossly misused and misunderstood political and media mantra. Among American human rights activists the word 'democracy' often refers to the responsibility of the majority to uphold the rights of

187 This is understood as "evangelism" by most Americans, but actually an important distinction exists between evangelism and proselytism.

188 Official policy states that the remains of non-Muslims who die in the kingdom must be repatriated to the country of origin, and there are complex rulings in the labour law for hiring non-Muslims to work there which lay down provisions for this potential eventuality. On the other hand, I have visited a highly guarded, private, clandestine cemetery where non-Muslims who died in the kingdom many years ago are buried. In more recent years, stillborn children have been buried there also.

all members of society, particularly minorities and underprivileged or dissenting groups, extending a civil responsibility of protecting the individual from the majority. This idea is incompatible within Islamic societies[189] simply because this concept is specifically derived from a secularist view of society and is rejected by many non-Western cultures.[190] Furthermore, the politicisation of the word 'democracy' over the past 30 years, and especially in respect to foreign military involvement in Iraq and Afghanistan over the past twenty-five years, has depreciated the value of the word in many parts of the world.

Democracy is a word that could simply refer to a political system that offers some degree of public participation in the political process, primarily in voting/elections. Otherwise, as in speeches referring to the promotion of democracy in Iraq, the word quite often has been used to refer more to a free-market economy than social freedoms. Fundamentally, secular democracy presumes that laws, values and the good of society are defined by the consensus of the majority of society's members – not by religious precepts. Secular democracy, therefore, is incompatible with Islam.[191]

Women in Islamic Society

The feminist movement in Western secular societies has elevated the status of women and provided educational, professional and social opportunities for women in ways that were inconceivable even 100 years ago. There is a strong motivation among Western women to share these developments with women in countries where those same opportunities do not yet exist. However, there are many conflicts of values to be considered when secular expectations regarding the role and rights of women in society are applied to Islamic culture. Moreover, the tension within Islamic societies that have adopted a more secular approach to social definition are also experiencing backlash relating to the role of women within their own societies, especially

---

189 Anna Marie Aagaard, 'Proselytism and Privacy: Some Reflections on the Tantur Conference on Religious Freedom', *Ecumenical Review*, 50, no. 4 (1998), 465.

190 Hille, 359. "The argument is that the emphasis on individualism in the West has no relevance to and presumably no validity in Asia where allegiance to the community is supposed to outweigh concern for the individual" (Hille, 153).

191 Please refer to Chapter 8 with particular emphasis on the concept of *shura*.

from Muslim women who reject values they see as non-Islamic.[192]

Islam presents the roles of man and woman in society as complementary, but not equal. Equality is perceived as an incorrect concept because it implies 'sameness'. Indeed, Muslim men *and* women would deny that men and women are equal. The difference is enshrined in the *Qur'an* in a number of places (ie. 2:282, 4:34).[193] Islam teaches that both roles are God-given and complementary because God has made man and woman differently; that both distinct roles are needed for the fulfillment of society and that they are not interchangeable. Even Muslim feminists, working for change and the improvement of the status of women in Islamic society, are heavily influenced by these principles from the *Sunnah*. This is a different kind of feminist movement than in America. The woman's place in society is indispensable and cannot be fulfilled by a man. She has a mandate from God to perpetuate the faith through her role as mother and source of nurture in the family.[194] The man's role is also indispensible, in that he provides for and protects the family, ensuring that the family's place in society is secure. Many Europeans and Americans would assert that we have 'moved on' from these 'restrictive' role orientations. It is essential to see that secular culture defines these roles as having originated from society, and are therefore open to change as society changes, while in Islam these roles are mandated by God himself and are therefore not open to change.

An additional issue in the discussion about human rights and the place of women in Islamic society one cannot ignore the ongoing debates about the right, obligation or oppression symbolised by the *hijab*. The *hijab* has become symbolic of women's rights among those who demand the right to wear the *hijab* and those who refuse to wear it. *Hijab* primarily reflects the concept of modesty.[195] In more recent times it has also come to reflect the politicisation of Islamic devotion both in Islamic countries and in other parts of the world. For Muslims in Europe or America a woman expresses, and preserves, her Islamic identity by wearing *hijab*. In a Muslim country,

---

192 Jane I Smith, 'Women in Islam: Equity, equality, and the search for the natural order', *Journal of the American Academy of Religion*, 47, 4 (1979), 528.

193 Hille, 356.

194 Haddad, 160.

195 Zuhur, 116.

a woman may choose to wear *hijab* as an expression of her commitment to living a truly Islamic lifestyle, much like an Evangelical Christian woman who always displays her 'Women's Aglow' lapel pin. [196] In other contexts, Muslim women are forced to wear *hijab* regardless of personal preference or religious conviction because of family or social pressure. Both of these manifestations emanate from a sense of need to project Islamic values and conformity, often as a specific rejection of non-Islamic influences perceived to have been imposed on the family or society from secularizing influences. When the issue is seen as the question of individual freedom for a woman to choose what she wears, it is a secular Western value. In essence, in Islamic countries the *hijab* question is more related to the sublimation of the individual to a society polarized by pro and anti secular trends rather than a question of individual human rights; whereas in America wearing the *hijab* represents, for Muslims, the freedom and their religious right to express their Islamic identity.

Freedom of Speech

It is almost impossible for the secularised Westerner to understand how strongly the honour of the family/community supersedes individuality in Islam. The extension of this concept culminates in the Islamic perception of the honour of Islam itself. Perhaps the most pressing *current* issue of difference and contention between values held dear by Westerners and values held by Muslims is the concept of freedom of speech/expression for the individual which thoroughly contradicts the Islamic concept of the individual's responsibility to conform to the values/laws of society. The proposal to burn a *Qur'an* in a public demonstration, the portrayal of Muhammad as a terrorist in a cartoon,[197] a NATO soldier using a *Qur'an* for target practice in Afghanistan, are news stories guaranteed to stimulate great anger among Muslims all over the world. As we have already seen in chapter eight, Islam requires a sense of social responsibility that supersedes the rights of the individual, rather than the responsibility to protect the rights of the individual.

---

196 Zuhur, 78.

197 Indeed, any portrayal of Muhammad in any form at all!

Protesting against perceived insult to the Prophet and Islam (lifted from the internet)

Christians in the West, who firmly accept the secular principle that freedom of speech entails freedom for one person to say and do things that could be considered to be offensive by another person, cannot grasp the depth of emotional reaction to events, publications, or statements insulting to Islam. The honour of Islam is a paramount consideration for all Muslims and actions such as those described above are considered to be immensely blasphemous. "The Muslim believes that it is obligatory to love the Companions of Allah's Messenger, and his family, and to honor them above all others."[198] In response to events like these, many Muslims feel honour-bound to join together with other Muslims to react in a public demonstration of Islamic identity and solidarity whenever a non-Muslim does something perceived as an insult to Islam. Some feel honour-bound to react in very strong, even violent ways. It is important to note that this reaction is not particularly understood to be a protest against the specific action reported in the news, but more as a statement to fellow Muslims about the sanctity of Islam, the *Qur'an*, the honour of the Prophet, and at the end of the day, the honour of the Islamic *Ummah*.

It is essential to many Muslims that they are seen by fellow Muslims to be supportive of the honour of Islam.[199] Indicative of this, in the past few years, and partly in response to these blasphemous events, different versions of 'bumper stickers' in Arabic have appeared in different countries of the Middle East expressing versions of sentiment like, "On the honour of my

---

198 Al-Jaza'iry, 29.

199 Wai-Yip Ho, 286.

mother and my father I will defend you, O my Prophet, to the death." and have become popular among conservative Muslims. It is always very unwise, in any conversation with Muslims, to make statements that could be perceived to criticise Islam, the *Qur'an*, or the person/prophet Muhammad, or even to express critical comparisons with Christian equivalents. Criticism, or worse – ridicule, of Islam, the Prophet, the *Qur'an*, is guaranteed to be received in a very negative way and is often interpreted as blasphemy. In many Islamic countries blasphemy laws carry the penalty of death. Blasphemy is a serious charge even in countries where the death penalty is not proscribed. The *Qur'anic* verse cited in respect to blasphemy is:

> *The punishment of those who wage war against God and His Apostle and strive with might and main for mischief through the land is; execution, or crucifixion, or the cutting of hands and feet from opposite sides, or exile from the land; that is their disgrace in this world and a heavy punishment is theirs in the hereafter* (Surah 5:36).

Blasphemy laws differ and vary in application in different Islamic countries but the laws do exist in most. In recent years, many implementations of the blasphemy laws in Pakistan have received considerable international attention because the judgments involved are inconsistent with international standards of justice. Sentences have seemed unduly severe, and many convictions seem more based on social pressure than any real evidence. In some significant cases, it is understood that blasphemy accusations are invoked simply as a sure-fire way of stirring up mass unrest to pressure local officials who are seen to be too secular.[200] It surely is one way of focusing the minds of local administrative officials as to the potential for political pressure from Islamic conservatives in their district. The main point here is recognition of the volatility of any subject or incident that could be perceived as threatening the honour of Islam. Regardless, not only the existence of blasphemy laws, but the way they are both debated and implemented give much insight into the importance of protecting the honour of Islam.

---

200 C, Toffolo, & C. Amjad-Ali, 'Christians in Pakistan confront charges of blasphemy', *Christian Century*, 115, 21 (1998), 717.

While issues of interaction and dialogue are probably more relevant for non-Muslims living in Arab Muslim cultures, they are also important for Christians who wish to interact with Arab Muslims living in Europe or the United States. With these pitfalls in mind, the next chapter will attempt to provide insight into approaches for conversations between Christians and Muslims – interfaith dialogue, both formal and incidental.

10. CHRISTIAN-MUSLIM DIALOGUE

Whereas the Christian partners in dialogue tend to be focused on theological issues and matters of religious pluralism (including the welfare of Christian minorities in Muslim majority countries), the concerns of the Muslim partners are quite different. They involve issues of socioeconomic justice and geopolitical crises that, for Christian dialogue partners, fall into the area of politics rather than religion.[201]

Islam and Christianity are both universal religions, and hold claims that are understood by many among the faithful to be mutually exclusive. Some see no purpose in dialog, but see interfaith encounters purely as opportunities to preach/convert. The evangelical component of Christianity is matched in Islam by *Allah's* command for *Da'wa*.[202] Interest in dialog is always motivated by a desire to be understood; but a conversation is not dialogue unless it also includes an interest or willingness to understand. It should be self-apparent that dialogue is only effective to the degree in which the communication is based on mutual understanding; and that better mutual understanding promotes deeper dialogue. Two one-way conversations happening at the same time in the same room is not dialogue; it's not even debate. Dialogue entails an openness to criticism, to critical analysis, to appreciation of what is admirable in each others' faith traditions; but it also must admit aspects of our own religious tradition that contribute to (or even promote) radical extremes, bigotry and violence. Real dialogue requires honesty, courage and vulnerability, critical introspection, identification of differences and a level of respect that gives room for those differences to co-exist.

The 9/11 event in the United States gave significant impetus among mainline Christians in America to be more aware of Islam in the USA and for many, to foster good relationships between Christians and Muslims in local communities. At the same time, and for many of the same reasons, Muslims in America are increasingly conscious of their public image and a need to present Islam in a positive light among non-Muslims. Religious leaders in both communities, agree that there is a great need to dispel misunderstanding

---

201 Ghulam-Haider Aasi, 'Christian-Muslim dialogue in the United States: a Muslim Perspective', *Currents in Theology and Mission*, 33, 3 (2007), 222.

202 Literally, to call people to religion. In practice it means to call people to Islam.

and negative stereotypes, to minimise demonisation of 'the other' and to be seen to be working together toward peaceful co-existence. However, efforts like these primarily address relatively baseline negative values. There is also a great need to determine positive purpose in dialogue, rather than settling for the use of dialogue simply as a methodology for reducing misunderstanding and even violence, as positive as that is, in its simplicity. Dialogue should accomplish more than simply distancing ourselves from others who are radical and embarrassing to both communities.

Too often, formal conversations between Muslims and Christians primarily seek to identify only what is held in common between two religious communities, attempting to reduce the discussion to recognition of sameness.[203] "We are all Americans." "We are all children of Abraham." "We all believe in one God." (See James 2:19!) Or, they can focus on areas of common concern and opportunity for mutual cooperation, like a faith-based day-care centre or English language tuition for immigrants. While these are healthy movements among peoples of different backgrounds who share community, this does not reflect dialogue in its deeper sense. Muslims and Christians, as citizens, should indeed work together to improve society and address needs in the community. It is always good for faith-based initiatives to be seen to be cooperative. Still, there is a difference between social/community cooperation and dialogue. Mutual respect cannot be based on ignorance; dialogue is more than getting to know each other and making friends. Real and honest dialogue requires identification of the distinctive features in our religious traditions that make us different.[204] The conversation lacks integrity if we ignore the fact that there are many values, traditions, and doctrines that distinguish us as very separate communities with very different traditions and values.[205] In today's world, Muslim/Christian dialogue is needed, but it must achieve more than simply find ways to co-exist despite our differences. True dialogue will always involve a learning process – a coming to know the dialogue partners on their own terms.

---

203 Nancy Fuchs-Kramer, 'Jews, Christians, and Muslims Face Modernity Together', *Journal of Ecumenical Studies*, 30, 3-4 (1993), 473.

204 "People in different cultures do not live in the same world with different labels attached to it, but in radically different worlds." Hiebert, 377.

205 Fuchs-Kramer, 473.

Concepts for Christians Interested in Promoting Dialogue

To return to the idea that dialogue is primarily motivated by the desire to be understood, and that for many it also includes the desire to understand, effective dialogue is by nature open-ended and without managed direction, and it develops over an extended period of time. Many Christians will approach dialogue as a theological opportunity, while most Muslims will look to dialogue as the best way to achieve security in the community. For example, immigrant Muslims in America are often, by social heritage, more globally aware and historically conscious than their non-Muslim neighbours. Americans, on the other hand, are unlikely to understand why the Crusader wars of 1000 years ago have any bearing on Muslims today. Most Americans are unaware of historic American foreign policy that has strengthened repressive regimes in Islamic countries.[206] Muslims in America rejoice in the personal and economic freedoms they enjoy in a secular democracy, but are uncomfortable with many secular freedoms that are permissive of immorality, and promote a level of individuality that contributes to social disintegration. And, of course, all of these concerns and many others are perceived in different ways among Christians and Muslims who are more secular in their life choices, or are more intentionally religious in their values. How does fruitful dialogue begin and flourish?

True dialogue involves attitude and process rather than a grasp of technique and a tightly defined programme with specified outcomes. Dialogue is, by nature, open-ended. It is as much a process of discovery as it is a process of building relationships. It will require learning to express oneself and one's beliefs in new ways, with new and different metaphors in order to be understood more fully, and it also involves learning appropriate metaphors that communicate accurately and clearly. The process is not unlike learning a language, which becomes most effective when one becomes able to think and dream in the new language. Christians and Muslims have much to learn about each other, and from each other.

In dialogue situations Americans (and Europeans) are perceived by

---

206 American support for Husni Mubarak over the past thirty years, while politically expedient, was viewed by many Egyptians as American complicity in oppression and corruption in direct opposition to the presentation of American values of Human Rights and Democratic principles.

Arab Muslims to be speaking from a position of strength. Economic predominance, military involvement in world affairs, and overwhelming influence in the mass media creates a strong sense of imbalance among peoples of other backgrounds.[207] Certainly immigrant communities inside the US or Europe don't see themselves as coming to any discussion from a position of strength. In fact, the general presentation in America or in Europe confirms the responsibility of the immigrant to learn the local values, history, local language and a general willingness to be assimilated into the local way of life. Immigrant Muslims generally feel they understand their adopted country while they do not feel understood themselves. In this context, Christians who wish to promote dialogue would do well to enter the process presenting an interest in learning from their Muslim counterparts. Like most people, most Muslims welcome the opportunity to present their views, concerns, traditions and culture.

What to Expect

Entering into dialogue as learners rather than teachers will certainly open an abundance of opportunity to clarify misperceptions and perspectives. This kind of open conversation will often take some time and many steps before any substantial, particularly theological, sharing takes place; or not at all. As noted above, Christians and Muslims are often looking for very different experiences in the name of dialogue. Most Muslims think they know about Christianity. In reality both Muslims and Christians hold many incorrect stereotypes about each other. Also, both Christians and Muslims will find it difficult to identify what is really religious and what is only cultural in the way they perceive their own faith, much less the faith of each other. The Christian will learn that different Muslims perceive Islam very differently, as different Christians will present Christianity very differently to Muslims. Many Muslims perceive Hollywood portrayals of dysfunctional families to be a reflection of Christianity (or at least Christian culture) while many Christians perceive oppression of women to be a main feature, or at least indicative, of Islamic culture. Each will be anxious to correct the misperceptions though it will be more difficult to comprehend

207 Khalid Durán, 'Jews, Christians, Muslims – Working Together for Modernity', *Journal of Ecumenical Studies,* 30, 3-4 (1993), 434.

and admit how much is and is not true in these perceptions.

Because meaningful dialogue is not about comprehending systems, the information shared in communication is secondary to the relationships established. After all, dialogue is about people understanding people, not an opportunity for polemic between religious paradigms. Participants will only be successful to the degree in which interpersonal trust is nurtured and strengthened. Like all friendships, some dialogue partners will 'get along' and understand each other better than others. Every person involved brings her/his personal history, prejudices and 'baggage' that influences the process. In other words, dialogue is more often frustrating than rewarding. It is important to remind yourself that it is the process that matters rather than any particular goal. Tangible "results" may not be apparent except in accidental or serendipitous outcomes.

What to expect? Expect to be challenged; expect to be changed. Expect to nurture friendships. Expect disappointments and frustration, and to be misunderstood. Expect God to move in the hearts of all who are honest in dialogue, and expect to gain a broader appreciation of how God moves in the lives of all whom he loves. True dialogue is an extension of our calling to carry an incarnational message of God's love to all people, especially those who live and believe differently than we do. After all, is this not a fulfilment of our mission as the followers of Christ?[208] In the conclusion we will explore how interaction with Islam can be a wonderful opportunity to deepen Christian faith, doctrine, and experience.

Modernity – satellite dishes on the roofs of apartment buildings in Baghdad, Iraq

208 1 Cor 9:18-23

11. CONCLUSION

"Why should humans love one another? Ultimately, because God is love. As Christians see things, God commands humans to love so that they can align their character with God's character. God's commands speak of God's character.[209]

Christians who wish to fulfil God's calling to live into the incarnation and resurrection, participate in the saving work of Jesus Christ, and manifest God's saving love to all the world have a difficult task indeed. Of course, the great Christological hymn of the incarnation in Philippians chapter two is written to encourage us to live selflessly in imitation of God's love for us.[210] As Christians, we too are exhorted to empty ourselves, have done with the old nature,[211] and be filled with the Spirit of God.[212] God became human, not because he did not understand humanity but to identify with his creation. I sincerely hope that this book has given insight and opportunity for many Christians to be more involved in this incarnational imperative as we look more deeply into knowing Arab Muslims as they wish to be known. It will require nothing short of an emptying of self if we wish to interact with Muslims in a truly open and loving relationship – to love as Christ has loved us. Twice in John's Gospel, (13:34 and 15:12), in the discourse at the last supper, his followers are asked to go WAY beyond loving their neighbour as they wish to be loved themselves.

It may seem too simple, but it is safe to say that there is a strong implication that salvation from what we would be without Christ involves becoming something, someone new. Imitating the incarnational initiative of God in Christ implies that we leave behind the self, the identity which does not reflect the love of God in Christ so that we can become; become a new person whose character is in itself a revelation of God's love in this broken world. It means that we see others as themselves, love them as themselves – not through our own self-perception and comfort zone (Romans, chapter

---

209 Volf, 105.

210 Brown, 795.

211 Rom 6:6; Rom 7:6; 1Cor 5:7-8; 2 Cor 5:17.

212 Rom 15:14; Eph 3:19; Col 1:9.

5). Sharing the love of Christ with others is not about methodology, or even a 'missiological breakthrough', but about character, about being a re-formed nature. It's more about relationship rather than about transmitting information. Living into our calling as Christians should be manifest in all of our relationships and our motivation to *be* in relationship. But, being in relationship with Muslims is a particular challenge for many Christians.

Popular trending presents the Christian-Muslim relationship context as confrontational, while the Gospel tells us it is an opportunity to move beyond our 'self' in an expression of love, acceptance and reconciliation, especially because the relationship is perceived by many Christians as hostile; also especially, because for many Muslims the relationship is perceived as confrontational. As Christians we are called to love others as they are, not as how we would wish them to be. It follows that the only way we can truly love any particular Muslim as Christ has loved us, the only way we could enter into a relationship with a Muslim which shows the love of Christ would entail entering into his/her world, just as Christ entered our world himself so that relationship between humanity and God could be restored.

Over the years I have lived in Arab Muslim cultures I have learned to appreciate and value many things that have diminished in my own American culture. The importance of family and community, the freedom to 'be religious' in all kinds of social interactions, the role of personal honour in business relationships are aspects of Islamic culture I admire. The study of Islam has also provided a wonderful platform to grow deeper in my understanding of Christian theology, particularly the incarnation and the trinity. I have learned that Christians can become so familiar with God that they have lost a sense of transcendence; but I have also seen that the fatherhood of God is an immensely undervalued expression of the teaching of Jesus – that God desires relationship with his creation; that God who is love manifests a vulnerability in his offer of love – an extreme vulnerability that includes death on a cross. Mostly, Islamic culture has taught me that we have little consciousness of how much of our own cultural values, even the secular values which try to distance religion from social interaction, are very deeply based on Christian theological roots.

Christians living among Muslims have a wonderful opportunity to come

Calligraphy – The Lord's Prayer beautifully presented in stylised Arabic script

to a fuller understanding of the wonder that God became human; that Jesus **is** 'the way the truth and the life';[213] that in Jesus it is God himself who is revealed to us. "For in him all the fullness of God was pleased to dwell, and through him God was pleased to reconcile to himself all things, whether on earth or in heaven, by making peace through the blood of his cross."[214] Experiencing the Islamic view of the *Qur'an* can help a casual Christian realise that the Bible is NOT a rulebook; Jesus is not a 'good

213 John 14:6

214 Col 1:19-20

teacher' or a prophet; salvation cannot be related to works but only to God's loving grace.

I have come to understand that in different ways many Christians are more like Muslims than they would care to admit, especially those who initially express their faith as belief in the Bible and see salvation as a result of reading, memorising and following the Bible as a rule book. This realisation has shaped my pastoral ministry in many, many ways. I will always remember hearing the Rev. Canon Dr. Kenneth Bailey, a good friend, say that many Christians see saving revelation as, "When God so loved the world he gave his only begotten book so that whosoever reads the book and believes the book shall have everlasting life." The experience of living in an Islamic culture presents a wonderful platform for turning this particular pastoral difficulty into an 'epiphany' for many in the daily ministry of parish work. It has led to many opportunities to help church members take a more critical look at what the Bible IS, and what it actually SAYS, rather than what we want it to say, or even what we have been taught it says.

For example, and with a bit of fun, let me point to one ubiquitous assimilation of Islam into Christian teaching and culture. Over and over through the years I have asked Christian friends about the story of Noah building the ark in the desert and people laughing at him. Never have I met a Christian who knew that this common Sunday School inheritance is not mentioned in the Genesis 6 story of Noah. It is, though, found in *Surah* 11 of the Qu'ran. I would like to do a study to try and trace how this tradition became so prominent among Christians, and how far back in history it actually goes!

In all, over the years of my ministry in the Middle East, I have been deeply enriched by living as a Christian grappling with Islamic values, pastoring Christians who grapple with the experience of Islamic culture and piety, and the insight I have gained through comparing/contrasting various aspects of Islamic and Middle Eastern culture with the cultures we read about in the Bible. The parables of Jesus in particular reflect brightly in that light. It is my hope that anyone who reads this text will be motivated to learn more about Islam, because in doing so they cannot help but learn more and more the depth of comfort and joy to be in a saving, loving relationship with God the Father through the incarnate Jesus Christ, enabled by the Holy Spirit to love others in the way we have been loved by him.

Life among Moslems [sic] *and contact with Islam compel the Christian to seek a deeper and more experiential knowledge of the Trinity as expressed in the ecumenical symbols of Christendom. The God whom men know outside of Jesus Christ and apart from the Holy Spirit is a nebulous thing; an idea and not a reality.*[215]

---

215 Samuel M Zwemer, 'The Allah of Islam and the God of Jesus Christ', *Theology today*, 3, 1 (1946), 75.

A Glossary of Islamic terms:

Abaya	A full-length, sleeveless outer garment worn by Arabs (usually understood as the outer garment worn by women).
Bid'a (or Bid'ah)	"Innovation." A practice or belief which was not present in Islam as it was revealed in the Koran, and established by the Sunnah on the basis of the Prophetic traditions.*
Bukra	Often used translated as "tomorrow" it more literally means, "early in the morning".† I find it more practical to translate *bukra* to mean something more like 'a time after today'.
Caliph	From the Arabic for "viceroy (of God)". The Caliph is the chief Muslim civil and religious ruler, regarded as the successor of Muhammad. (The caliph ruled in Baghdad until 1258 and then in Egypt until the Ottoman conquest of 1517; the title was then held by the Ottoman sultans until it was abolished in 1924 by Atatürk.)
Da' wa	Qur'anically, the word most commonly means to invoke the deity, and so to place one's faith in that deity. It also means to call to religion, and in this sense Muhammad is a *da'i* or caller. Today it usually means missionary work to bring new believers to Islam or to reinforce belief.*
Dar al Islam (Darassalam)	(Lit. the abode of peace"). Territories in which Islam and the Islamic religious Law (the *Shari'a*) prevail.*
Deism	Belief in the existence of a supreme being, specifically of a creator who does not intervene in the universe. The term is used chiefly of an intellectual movement of the 17th and 18th centuries that accepted the existence of a creator on the basis of reason but rejected belief in a supernatural deity who interacts with humankind.

Dhimmi	A person belonging to the category of "protected people" (ahl ad-dhimmah) in the Islamic state. In classical times, these were the recognized monotheists: Jews, Christians, and "Sabians", who were granted autonomy of institutions and protection under Islam. In return they were required to pay a head tax (jizyah), and an exemption tax (kharaj).*
Djinn	An intelligent spirit of lower rank than the angels, able to appear in human and animal forms and to possess humans. (Plural = Djinni *or* Genie.)
Ekklesia	A Greek word which is often translated "church" in referring to both the particularity of the small and local as well as the generality of the universal (in space and time) community of people reconciled to God in Jesus Christ.
Hadith	A collection of traditions containing sayings of the prophet Muhammad that, with accounts of his daily practice (the Sunnah), constitute the major source of guidance for Muslims apart from the Qur'an.
Halal	Religiously acceptable according to Muslim law.
Haram	Forbidden or proscribed by Islamic law.
Hijab	(Lit. a "veil" or "partition.) A common meaning of *hijab* today is the adherence to certain standards of modest dress for women.*
Hijra	Muhammad's departure from Mecca to Medina in ad 622, prompted by the opposition of the merchants of Mecca and marking the consolidation of the first Muslim community.
Ijma	(Lit. 'assembly'.) One of the principles of Islamic law. Its basis is the *Hadith*: "my community shall never be in agreement in error".*
Ijtihad	Diligence, industry, industriousness, exertion, effort, endeavour, persistence (and other synonyms).†

Imam	A title of various Muslim leaders, especially of one succeeding Muhammad as leader of Shiite Islam.
Islam	From the Arabic *'islām* meaning 'submission,' from '*aslama* 'submit (to God).'
Jahiliyyah	From the Arabic *jahil*, meaning "ignorant, "untaught." The time of ignorance or period of Arab paganism preceding the revelation of Islam.*
Jihad	From the Arabic *jihād*, literally meaning '*effort*', expressing in Muslim thought the struggle on behalf of God and Islam. (This is not unlike the way the word "crusade" is often used in the West.)
Kor'an	Or Koran, See Qur'an (an alternate transliteration of the Arabic).
Madhhab	(Lit. a "direction"; pl. *madhābib*.) A system of thought, an intellectual approach. Specifically, the term madhhab is used to refer to each of the schools of law.*
Mujahidin	From the Persian and Arabic *mujāhidīn*, colloquial plural of *mujāhid*, denoting a person who fights a jihad.
Mujtahid	(Lit. "one who strives"; pl. *mujtahidūn*.) An authority who makes original decisions of canon law, rather than applying precedents already established.
Qur'an	The Islamic sacred book, believed to be the word of God as dictated to Muhammad by the archangel Gabriel and written down in Arabic. The Koran consists of 114 units of varying lengths, known as *suras*; the first *surah* is said as part of the ritual prayer. These touch upon all aspects of human existence, including matters of doctrine, social organisation, and legislation. See also Kor'an.
Secular	Denoting attitudes, activities, or other things that have no religious or spiritual basis. Contrasted with sacred.

Shahadah	The Muslim profession of faith ("There is no god but Allah, and Muhammad is the messenger of Allah"). The *shahadah* involves both perceiving and declaring that "there is no god but God".
Shari'a	Islamic canonical law based on the teachings of the Koran and the traditions of the Prophet (Hadith and Sunnah), prescribing both religious and secular duties and sometimes retributive penalties for law breaking. It has generally been supplemented by legislation adapted to the conditions of the day, though the manner in which it should be applied in modern states is a subject of dispute between Islamic fundamentalists and modernists.
Shi'a	One of the two main branches of Islam (followed esp. in Iran) that rejects the first three Sunni caliphs and regards Ali, the fourth caliph, as Muhammad's first true successor.
Shirk	The "association" of something with God, other than God Himself. Islam considers *shirk* to be the fundamental error at the root of all sin or transgression.
Shura	The principle of consultation, in particular as applied to government.
Surah	A chapter or section of the Qu'ran.
Sunnah	The traditional portion of Muslim law based on Muhammad's words or acts, accepted (together with the Qur'an) as authoritative by Muslims and followed particularly by Sunni Muslims.
Sunni	One of the two main branches of Islam, commonly described as orthodox, and differing from Shia in its understanding of the Sunnah and in its acceptance of the first three caliphs.

Taqleed	In religious matters it is the opposite of ijtihad, the pursuit of original solutions to questions; in law it is the reliance upon the decisions and precedents set in the past.*
Tawheed	To declare or acknowledge oneness. The acknowledging of the Unity of God, the indivisible, Absolute, and the sole Real.*
Ummah	The whole community of Muslims bound together by ties of religion.
Wahabi	A strictly orthodox Sunni Muslim sect founded by Muhammad ibn Abd al-Wahhab (1703-92). This sect advocates a return to the early Islam of the Koran and Sunnah, rejecting later innovations; the sect is still the predominant religious force in Saudi Arabia.

Unmarked definitions are taken from New Oxford American Dictionary, 2005-2009 Apple Inc. {Version 2.1.1 (80.1)}.

* Marked definitions are taken from Cyril Glassé, *The New Encyclopedia of Islam*, Rev. ed. (Walnut Creek, CA: AltaMira Press, 2001).

† Marked definitions are taken from Rohi Baalbaki, *Al Mawrid – A Modern Arabic – English Dictionary*, (Beirut Lebanon: Dar El-Ilm Lilmalayin, 1988).

Appendix 1

Many books, movies, and articles are produced for popular consumption. They are produced with commercial viability in mind more than historic, cultural or sociological accuracy. I've read many fascinating books based on historic events or popularly held 'truisms' which have been informative, but have left me with distorted perceptions of the actual reality portrayed. Many readers will remember the disorientation among believing Christians that resulted from the hugely popular book, *The Da Vinci Code* by Dan Brown. In my pastoral role I had to remind many readers that the book is a novel, that the introduction stating that it is based on true events is also part of the novel... The productions listed on the left fall into this category, while the books listed in the right are suggestions of corrective reading.

Non-Helpful	Helpful
Uris, Leon, *The Haj* (New York: Doubleday, 1984) Uris, Leon, *Exodus* (New York: Doubleday, 1958)	Chapman, Colin. *Whose Promised Land?* New updated ed. A Lion Paperback. Oxford (Batavia, Ill.: Lion Pub., 1992)
"Pastor" Terry Jones; Youtube video *The Innocent Prophet,* denigrating the prophet Muhammad: http://www.youtube.com/watch?feature=player_embedded&v=7gwcuG2jb9k&bpctr=1356013858&bpctr=1364636946&bpctr=1364636953&bpctr=1364636959	Lings, Martin. *Muhammad : His Life Based on the Earliest Sources* (London: Islamic Texts Society: Allen & Unwin, 1983) Watt, W. Montgomery. *Muhammad: Prophet and Statesman* A Galaxy Book, (Oxford: Oxford University Press, 1974)
Hitchcock, Mark, *Middle East Burning* (Eugene, Or.: Harvest House Publishers, 2012) Genger, Ross W., *Allah is not God and Muhammad is the Messenger of Allah* (Bloomington, Indiana: Xlibris Corp, 2010)	Abd-Allah, Umar F.,'Do Christians and Muslims worship the same God?' *Christian Century,* 121, 17 (August 2004) Zwemer, Samuel Marinus, 'The Allah of Islam and the God of Jesus Christ', *Theology Today,* 3, 1 (April 1946)

Non-Helpful	Helpful
Sasson, Jean, *Daughters of Arabia* (London: Bantam Books, 1994)	Mernissi, Fatima, *Beyond the Veil: Male-Female Dynamics in Modern Muslim Society*, rev. ed. (Bloomington: Indiana University Press, 1987)
Alsanea, Rajaa, *Girls of Riyadh* (New York: Penguin Books, 2008) (Evocative, but it IS a novel – not a true story)	Alireza, Marianne, *At the Drop of a Veil / Marianne Alireza* (Costa Mesa, Calif.: Blind Owl Press, 2002)
Feiler, Bruce, *Abraham: A Journey to the Heart of Three Faiths* (New York: William Morrow, 2002) (Reductionist portrayal. Sentiment with not much content)	Cragg, Kenneth, *Troubled by Truth: Biographies in the Presence of Mystery* (Cleveland, Ohio: Pilgrim Press, 1994)

Appendix 2

Universal Islamic Declaration of Human Rights
21 Dhul Qaidah 1401 – 19 September 1981

Contents

This is a declaration for mankind, a guidance and instruction to those who fear God. (Al Qur'an, Al-Imran 3:138)

Foreword

Islam gave to mankind an ideal code of human rights fourteen centuries ago. These rights aim at conferring honour and dignity on mankind and eliminating exploitation, oppression and injustice.

Human rights in Islam are firmly rooted in the belief that God, and God alone, is the Law Giver and the Source of all human rights. Due to their Divine origin, no ruler, government, assembly or authority can curtail or violate in any way the human rights conferred by God, nor can they be surrendered.

Human rights in Islam are an integral part of the overall Islamic order and it is obligatory on all Muslim governments and organs of society to implement them in letter and in spirit within the framework of that order.

It is unfortunate that human rights are being trampled upon with impunity in many countries of the world, including some Muslim countries. Such violations are a matter of serious concern and are arousing the conscience of more and more people throughout the world.

I sincerely hope that this Declaration of Human Rights will give a powerful impetus to the Muslim peoples to stand firm and defend resolutely and courageously the rights conferred on them by God.

This Declaration of Human Rights is the second fundamental document proclaimed by the Islamic Council to mark the beginning of the 15th Century of the Islamic era, the first being the Universal Islamic Declaration announced at the International Conference on The Prophet Muhammad (peace and blessings be upon him) and his Message, held in London from 12 to 15 April 1980.

The Universal Islamic Declaration of Human Rights is based on the Qur'an and the Sunnah and has been compiled by eminent Muslim scholars, jurists and representatives of Islamic movements and thought. May God reward them all for their efforts and guide us along the right path.

Paris 21 Dhul Qaidah 1401 Salem Azzam 19th September 1981 Secretary General

O men! Behold, We have created you all out of a male and a female, and

have made you into nations and tribes, so that you might come to know one another. Verily, the noblest of you in the sight of God is the one who is most deeply conscious of Him. Behold, God is all-knowing, all aware. (Al Qur'an, Al-Hujurat 49:13)

Preamble

WHEREAS the age-old human aspiration for a just world order wherein people could live, develop and prosper in an environment free from fear, oppression, exploitation and deprivation, remains largely unfulfilled;

WHEREAS the Divine Mercy unto mankind reflected in its having been endowed with super-abundant economic sustenance is being wasted, or unfairly or unjustly withheld from the inhabitants of the earth;

WHEREAS Allah (God) has given mankind through His revelations in the Holy Qur'an and the Sunnah of His Blessed Prophet Muhammad an abiding legal and moral framework within which to establish and regulate human institutions and relationships;

WHEREAS the human rights decreed by the Divine Law aim at conferring dignity and honour on mankind and are designed to eliminate oppression and injustice;

WHEREAS by virtue of their Divine source and sanction these rights can neither be curtailed, abrogated or disregarded by authorities, assemblies or other institutions, nor can they be surrendered or alienated;

Therefore we, as Muslims, who believe

a) in God, the Beneficent and Merciful, the Creator, the Sustainer, the Sovereign, the sole Guide of mankind and the Source of all Law;

b) in the Vicegerency (Khalifah) of man who has been created to fulfill the Will of God on earth;

c) in the wisdom of Divine guidance brought by the Prophets, whose mission found its culmination in the final Divine message that was conveyed by the Prophet Muhammad (Peace be upon him) to all mankind;

d) that rationality by itself without the light of revelation from God can neither be a sure guide in the affairs of mankind nor provide spiritual nourishment to the human soul, and, knowing that the teachings of Islam represent the quintessence of Divine guidance in its final and perfect form, feel duty-bound to remind man of the high status and dignity bestowed on him by God;

e) in inviting all mankind to the message of Islam;

f) that by the terms of our primeval covenant with God our duties and obligations have priority over our rights, and that each one of us is under a bounden duty to spread the teachings of Islam by word, deed, and indeed in all gentle ways, and to make them effective not only in our individual lives but also in the society around us;

g) in our obligation to establish an Islamic order:

  i) wherein all human beings shall be equal and none shall enjoy a privilege or suffer a disadvantage or discrimination by reason of race, colour, sex, origin or language;

  ii) wherein all human beings are born free;

  iii) wherein slavery and forced labour are abhorred;

  iv) wherein conditions shall be established such that the institution of family shall be preserved, protected and honoured as the basis of all social life;

  v) wherein the rulers and the ruled alike are subject to, and equal before, the Law;

  vi) wherein obedience shall be rendered only to those commands that are in consonance with the Law;

  vii) wherein all worldly power shall be considered as a sacred trust, to be exercised within the limits prescribed by the Law and in a manner approved by it, and with due regard for the priorities fixed by it;

  viii) wherein all economic resources shall be treated as Divine blessings bestowed upon mankind, to be enjoyed by all in accordance with the rules and the values set out in the Qur'an and the Sunnah;

ix) wherein all public affairs shall be determined and conducted, and the authority to administer them shall be exercised after mutual consultation (Shura) between the believers qualified to contribute to a decision which would accord well with the Law and the public good;

x) wherein everyone shall undertake obligations proportionate to his capacity and shall be held responsible pro rata for his deeds;

xi) wherein everyone shall, in case of an infringement of his rights, be assured of appropriate remedial measures in accordance with the Law;

xii) wherein no one shall be deprived of the rights assured to him by the Law except by its authority and to the extent permitted by it;

xiii) wherein every individual shall have the right to bring legal action against anyone who commits a crime against society as a whole or against any of its members;

xiv) wherein every effort shall be made to

(a) secure unto mankind deliverance from every type of exploitation, injustice and oppression,

(b) ensure to everyone security, dignity and liberty in terms set out and by methods approved and within the limits set by the Law;

Do hereby, as servants of Allah and as members of the Universal Brotherhood of Islam, at the beginning of the Fifteenth Century of the Islamic Era, affirm our commitment to uphold the following inviolable and inalienable human rights that we consider are enjoined by Islam.

I Right to Life

a) Human life is sacred and inviolable and every effort shall be made to protect it. In particular no one shall be exposed to injury or death, except under the authority of the Law.

b) Just as in life, so also after death, the sanctity of a person's body shall be inviolable. It is the obligation of believers to see that a deceased person's body is handled with due solemnity.

II Right to Freedom

a) Man is born free. No inroads shall be made on his right to liberty except under the authority and in due process of the Law.

b) Every individual and every people has the inalienable right to freedom in all its forms; physical, cultural, economic and political – and shall be entitled to struggle by all available means against any infringement or abrogation of this right; and every oppressed individual or people has a legitimate claim to the support of other individuals and/or peoples in such a struggle.

III Right to Equality and Prohibition Against Impermissible Discrimination

a) All persons are equal before the Law and are entitled to equal opportunities and protection of the Law.

b) All persons shall be entitled to equal wage for equal work.

c) No person shall be denied the opportunity to work or be discriminated against in any manner or exposed to greater physical risk by reason of religious belief, colour, race, origin, sex or language.

IV Right to Justice

a) Every person has the right to be treated in accordance with the Law, and only in accordance with the Law.

b) Every person has not only the right but also the obligation to protest against injustice; to recourse to remedies provided by the Law in respect of any unwarranted personal injury or loss; to self-defence against any charges that are preferred against him and to obtain fair adjudication before an independent judicial tribunal in any dispute with public authorities or any other person.

c) It is the right and duty of every person to defend the rights of any other person and the community in general (Hisbah).

d) No person shall be discriminated against while seeking to defend private and public rights.

e) It is the right and duty of every Muslim to refuse to obey any command which is contrary to the Law, no matter by whom it may be issued.

V Right to Fair Trial

a) No person shall be adjudged guilty of an offence and made liable to punishment except after proof of his guilt before an independent judicial tribunal.

b) No person shall be adjudged guilty except after a fair trial and after reasonable opportunity for defence has been provided to him.

c) Punishment shall be awarded in accordance with the Law, in proportion to the seriousness of the offence and with due consideration of the circumstances under which it was committed.

d) No act shall be considered a crime unless it is stipulated as such in the clear wording of the Law.

e) Every individual is responsible for his actions. Responsibility for a crime cannot be vicariously extended to other members of his family or group, who are not otherwise directly or indirectly involved in the commission of the crime in question.

VI Right to Protection Against Abuse of Power

Every person has the right to protection against harassment by official agencies. He is not liable to account for himself except for making a defence to the charges made against him or where he is found in a situation wherein a question regarding suspicion of his involvement in a crime could be reasonably raised

VII Right to Protection Against Torture

No person shall be subjected to torture in mind or body, or degraded, or threatened with injury either to himself or to anyone related to or held dear by him, or forcibly made to confess to the commission of a crime, or forced to consent to an act which is injurious to his interests.

VIII Right to Protection of Honour and Reputation

Every person has the right to protect his honour and reputation against calumnies, groundless charges or deliberate attempts at defamation and blackmail.

IX Right to Asylum

a) Every persecuted or oppressed person has the right to seek refuge and asylum. This right is guaranteed to every human being irrespective of race, religion, colour and sex.

b) Al Masjid Al Haram (the sacred house of Allah) in Mecca is a sanctuary for all Muslims.

X Rights of Minorities

a) The Qur'anic principle "There is no compulsion in religion" shall govern the religious rights of non-Muslim minorities.

b) In a Muslim country religious minorities shall have the choice to be governed in respect of their civil and personal matters by Islamic Law, or by their own laws.

XI Right and Obligation to Participate in the Conduct and Management of Public Affairs

a) Subject to the Law, every individual in the community (Ummah) is entitled to assume public office.

b) Process of free consultation (Shura) is the basis of the administrative relationship between the government and the people. People also have the right to choose and remove their rulers in accordance with this principle.

XII Right to Freedom of Belief, Thought and Speech

a) Every person has the right to express his thoughts and beliefs so long as he remains within the limits prescribed by the Law. No one, however, is entitled to disseminate falsehood or to circulate reports which may outrage public decency, or to indulge in slander, innuendo or to cast defamatory aspersions on other persons.

b) Pursuit of knowledge and search after truth is not only a right but a duty of every Muslim.

c) It is the right and duty of every Muslim to protest and strive (within the limits set out by the Law) against oppression even if it involves challenging the highest authority in the state.

d) There shall be no bar on the dissemination of information provided it does not endanger the security of the society or the state and is confined within the limits imposed by the Law.

e) No one shall hold in contempt or ridicule the religious beliefs of others or incite public hostility against them; respect for the religious feelings of others is obligatory on all Muslims.

XIII Right to Freedom of Religion

Every person has the right to freedom of conscience and worship in accordance with his religious beliefs.

XIV Right to Free Association

a) Every person is entitled to participate individually and collectively in the religious, social, cultural and political life of his community and to establish institutions and agencies meant to enjoin what is right (ma'roof) and to prevent what is wrong (munkar).

b) Every person is entitled to strive for the establishment of institutions whereunder an enjoyment of these rights would be made possible. Collectively, the community is obliged to establish conditions so as to allow its members full development of their personalities.

XV The Economic Order and the Rights Evolving Therefrom

a) In their economic pursuits, all persons are entitled to the full benefits of nature and all its resources. These are blessings bestowed by God for the benefit of mankind as a whole.

b) All human beings are entitled to earn their living according to the Law.

c) Every person is entitled to own property individually or in association with others. State ownership of certain economic resources in the public interest is legitimate.

d) The poor have the right to a prescribed share in the wealth of the rich, as fixed by Zakah, levied and collected in accordance with the Law.

e) All means of production shall be utilised in the interest of the community (Ummah) as a whole, and may not be neglected or misused.

f) In order to promote the development of a balanced economy and to protect society from exploitation, Islamic Law forbids monopolies, unreasonable restrictive trade practices, usury, the use of coercion in the making of contracts and the publication of misleading advertisements.

g) All economic activities are permitted provided they are not detrimental to the interests of the community (Ummah) and do not violate Islamic laws and values.

XVI Right to Protection of Property

No property may be expropriated except in the public interest and on payment of fair and adequate compensation.

XVII Status and Dignity of Workers

Islam honours work and the worker and enjoins Muslims not only to treat the worker justly but also generously. He is not only to be paid his earned wages promptly, but is also entitled to adequate rest and leisure.

XVIII Right to Social Security

Every person has the right to food, shelter, clothing, education and medical care consistent with the resources of the community. This obligation of the community extends in particular to all individuals who cannot take care of themselves due to some temporary or permanent disability.

XIX Right to Found a Family and Related Matters

a) Every person is entitled to marry, to found a family and to bring up children in conformity with his religion, traditions and culture. Every spouse is entitled to such rights and privileges and carries such obligations as are stipulated by the Law.

b) Each of the partners in a marriage is entitled to respect and consideration from the other.

c) Every husband is obligated to maintain his wife and children according to his means.

d) Every child has the right to be maintained and properly brought up by its parents, it being forbidden that children are made to work at an early age or that any burden is put on them which would arrest or harm their natural development.

e) If parents are for some reason unable to discharge their obligations towards a child it becomes the responsibility of the community to fulfill these obligations at public expense.

f) Every person is entitled to material support, as well as care and protection, from his family during his childhood, old age or incapacity. Parents are entitled to material support as well as care and protection from their children.

g) Motherhood is entitled to special respect, care and assistance on the part of the family and the public organs of the community (Ummah).

h) Within the family, men and women are to share in their obligations and responsibilities according to their sex, their natural endowments, talents and inclinations, bearing in mind their common responsibilities toward their progeny and their relatives.

i) No person may be married against his or her will, or lose or suffer diminution of legal personality on account of marriage.

XX Rights of Married Women

Every married woman is entitled to:

a) live in the house in which her husband lives;

b) receive the means necessary for maintaining a standard of living which is not inferior to that of her spouse, and, in the event of divorce, receive during the statutory period of waiting (iddah) means of maintenance commensurate with her husband's resources, for herself as well as for the children she nurses or keeps, irrespective of her own financial status, earnings, or property that she may hold in her own rights;

c) seek and obtain dissolution of marriage (Khul'a) in accordance with the terms of the Law. This right is in addition to her right to seek divorce through the courts.

d) inherit from her husband, her parents, her children and other relatives according to the Law;

e) strict confidentiality from her spouse, or ex-spouse if divorced, with regard to any information that he may have obtained about her, the disclosure of which could prove detrimental to her interests. A similar responsibility rests upon her in respect of her spouse or ex-spouse.

XXI Right to Education

a) Every person is entitled to receive education in accordance with his natural capabilities.

b) Every person is entitled to a free choice of profession and career and to the opportunity for the full development of his natural endowments.

XXII Right of Privacy

Every person is entitled to the protection of his privacy.

XXIII Right to Freedom of Movement and Residence

a) In view of the fact that the World of Islam is veritably Ummah Islamia, every Muslim shall have the right to freely move in and out of any Muslim country.

b) No one shall be forced to leave the country of his residence, or be arbitrarily deported therefrom without recourse to due process of Law.

Explanatory Notes

1 In the above formulation of Human Rights, unless the context provides otherwise:

   a) the term 'person' refers to both the male and female sexes.

   b) the term 'Law' denotes the Shari'a, i.e. the totality of ordinances derived from the Qur'an and the Sunnah and any other laws that are deduced from these two sources by methods considered valid in Islamic jurisprudence.

2 Each one of the Human Rights enunciated in this declaration carries a corresponding duty.

3 In the exercise and enjoyment of the rights referred to above every person shall be subject only to such limitations as are enjoined by the Law for the purpose of securing the due recognition of, and respect for, the rights and the freedom of others and of meeting the just requirements of morality, public order and the general welfare of the Community (Ummah).

The Arabic text of this Declaration is the original.

Glossary of Arabic Terms

SUNNAH	The example or way of life of the Prophet (peace be upon him), embracing what he said, did or agreed to.
KHALIFAH	The vicegerency of man on earth or succession to the Prophet, transliterated into English as the Caliphate.
HISBAH	Public vigilance, an institution of the Islamic State enjoined to observe and facilitate the fulfillment of right norms of public behaviour. The "Hisbah" consists in public vigilance as well as an opportunity to private individuals to seek redress through it.
MA'ROOF	Good act.
MUNKAR	Reprehensible deed.

ZAKAH	The 'purifying' tax on wealth, one of the five pillars of Islam obligatory on Muslims.
'IDDAH	The waiting period of a widowed or divorced woman during which she is not to re-marry.
KHUL'A	Divorce a woman obtains at her own request.
UMMAH ISLAMIA	World Muslim community.
SHARI'A	Islamic law.

References

Note: The Roman numerals refer to the topics in the text.
The Arabic numerals refer to the Chapter and the Verse of the Qur'an, i.e. 5:32 means Chapter 5, Verse 32.

1 1 Qur'an Al-Maidah 5:32
2 Hadith narrated by Muslim, Abu Daud,Tirmidhi, Nasai
3 Hadith narrated by Bukhari II
4 Hadith narrated by Bukhari, Muslim
5 Sayings of Caliph Umar
6 Qur'an As-Shura 42:41
7 Qur'an Al-Hajj 22:41 III
8 From the Prophet's address
9 Hadith narrated by Bukhari, Muslim, Abu Daud, Tirmidhi, Nasai
10 From the address of Caliph Abu Bakr
11 From the Prophet's farewell address
12 Qur'an Al-Ahqaf 46:19
13 Hadith narrated by Ahmad
14 Qur'an Al-Mulk 67:15
15 Qur'an Al-Zalzalah 99:7-8
16 Qur'an An-Nisa 4:59
17 Qur'an Al-Maidah 5:49
18 Qur'an An-Nisa 4:148
19 Hadith narrated by Bukhari, Muslim, Tirmidhi
20 Hadith narrated by Bukhari, Muslim
21 Hadith narrated by Muslim, Abu Daud, Tirmdhi, Nasai

22 Hadith narrated by Bukhari, Muslim, Abu Daud, Tirmidhi, Nasai
23 Hadith narrated by Abu Daud, Tirmidhi
24 Hadith narrated by Bukhari, Muslim, Abu Daud, Tirmidhi, Nasai
25 Hadith narrated by Bukhari V
26 Hadith narrated by Bukhari, Muslim
27 Qur'an Al-Isra 17:15
28 Qur'an Al-Ahzab 33:5
29 Qur'an Al-Hujurat 49:6
30 Qur'an An-Najm 53:28
31 Qur'an Al Baqarah 2:229
32 Hadith narrated by Al Baihaki, Hakim
33 Qur'an Al-Isra 17:15
34 Qur'an At-Tur 52:21
35 Qur'an Yusuf 12:79 VI
36 Qur'an Al Ahzab 33:58 VII
37 Hadith narrated by Bukhari, Muslim, Abu Daud, Tirmidhi, Nasai
38 Hadith narrated by Ibn Majah VIII
39 From the Prophet's farewell address
40 Qur'an Al-Hujurat 49:12
41 Qur'an Al-Hujurat 49:11 IX
42 Qur'an At-Tawba 9:6
43 Qur'an Al-Imran 3:97
44 Qur'an Al-Baqarah 2:125
45 Qur'an Al-Hajj 22:25 X
46 Qur'an Al Baqarah 2:256
47 Qur'an Al-Maidah 5:42
48 Qur'an Al-Maidah 5:43
49 Qur'an Al-Maidah 5:47 XI
50 Qur'an As-Shura 42:38
51 Hadith narrated by Ahmad
52 From the address of Caliph Abu Bakr XII
53 Qur'an Al-Ahzab 33:60-61
54 Qur'an Saba 34:46
55 Hadith narrated by Tirmidhi, Nasai
56 Qur'an An-Nisa 4:83

57 Qur'an Al-Anam 6:108 XIII
58 Qur'an Al Kafirun 109:6 XIV
59 Qur'an Yusuf 12:108
60 Qur'an Al-Imran 3:104
61 Qur'an Al-Maidah 5:2
62 Hadith narrated by Abu Daud, Tirmidhi,Nasai, Ibn Majah XV
63 Qur'an Al-Maidah 5:120
64 Qur'an Al-Jathiyah 45:13
65 Qur'an Ash-Shuara 26:183
66 Qur'an Al-Isra 17:20
67 Qur'an Hud 11:6
68 Qur'an Al-Mulk 67:15
69 Qur'an An-Najm 53:48
70 Qur'an Al-Hashr 59:9
71 Qur'an Al-Maarij 70:24-25
72 Sayings of Caliph Abu Bakr
73 Hadith narrated by Bukhari, Muslim
74 Hadith narrated by Muslim
75 Hadith narrated by Muslim, Abu Daud,Tirmidhi, Nasai
76 Hadith narrated by Bukhari, Muslim, Abu Daud, Tirmidhi, Nasai
77 Qur'an Al-Mutaffifin 83:1-3
78 Hadith narrated by Muslim
79 Qur'an Al-Baqarah 2:275
80 Hadith narrated by Bukhari, Muslim,Abu Daud, Tirmidhi, Nasai XVI
81 Qur'an Al Baqarah 2:188
82 Hadith narrated by Bukhari
83 Hadith narrated by Muslim
84 Hadith narrated by Muslim, Tirmidhi XVII
85 Qur'an At-Tawbah 9:105
86 Hadith narrated by Abu Yala Majma Al Zawaid
87 Hadith narrated by Ibn Majah
88 Qur'an Al-Ahqaf 46:19
89 Qur'an At-Tawbah 9:105
90 Hadith narrated by Tabarani Majma Al Zawaid
91 Hadith narrated by Bukhari XVIII
92 Qur'an Al-Ahzab 33:6 XIX

93 Qur'an An-Nisa 4:1
94 Qur'an Al-Baqarah 2:228
95 Hadith narrated by Bukhari, Muslim,Abu Daud, Tirmidhi, Nasai
96 Qur'an Ar-Rum 30:21
97 Qur'an At-Talaq 65:7
98 Qur'an Al-Isra 17:24
99 Hadith narrated by Bukhari, Muslim, Abu Daud, Tirmidhi
100 Hadith narrated by Abu Daud
101 Hadith narrated by Bukhari, Muslim
102 Hadith narrated by Abu Daud, Tirmidhi
103 Hadith narrated by Ahmad, Abu Daud XX
104 Qur'an At-Talaq 65:6
105 Qur'an An-Nisa 4:34
106 Qur'an At-Talaq 65:6
107 Qur'an AtTalaq 65:6
108 Qur'an Al-Baqarah 2:229
109 Qur'an An-Nisa 4:12
110 Qur'an Al-Baqarah 2:237 XXI
111 Qur'an Al-Isra 17:23-24
112 Hadith narrated by Ibn Majah
113 Qur'an Al-Imran 3:187
114 From the Prophet's farewell address
115 Hadith narrated by Bukhari, Muslim
116 Hadith narrated by Bukhari, Muslim, Abu Daud, Tirmidhi XXII
117 Hadith narrated by Muslim
118 Qur'an Al-Hujurat 49:12
119 Hadith narrated by Abu Daud, Tirmidhi XXIII
120 Qur'an Al-Mulk 67:15
121 Qur'an Al-Anam 6:11
122 Qur'an An-Nisa 4:97
123 Qur'an Al-Baqarah 2:217
124 Qur'an Al-Hashr 59:9

Published by: Islamic Council, 16 Grosvenor Crescent, London SW1X 7EP

Appendix 3

Islam and Corruption of Scriptures*

It would be interesting to explore what is meant by Qur'anic confirmation of the earlier Scriptures. An influential contemporary scholar, Mawdudi, for instance, elaborates the Islamic viewpoint on the question. He claims that the Qur'anic confirmation of the Evangel and the Torah (see 3:3, and elsewhere) does not mean confirmation of all the contents of the four Gospels and/or the contents of the first five books of the Old Testament. For Evangel cannot be equated with the four Gospels, nor Torah with the five books of the Old Testament, though the former are embodied in the latter. After some historical discussion of Torah, Mawdudi points out that the five books have a biographical-historical character, and the fragments of the Torah are scattered over those five books. The fragments which open with Moses saying "Thus saith the Lord" are presumably part of the Torah referred to by the Qur'an. Because of the exegetical interpolations, it is difficult for the lay reader to be able to distinguish the fragments of the original Torah from the human interpolations, but it is not difficult for a person who has an insight into the Scriptural literature to sift them to some extent. The Qur'an confirms only these fragments, and, indeed, were they to be brought together, one would notice no difference between the teachings embodied in them and in the Qur'an. And if a few differences are noticeable, they would be regarding the legal *minutiae*. Likewise, the Evangel mentioned in the Qur'an comprises the inspired sermons and sayings of Jesus as a prophet during the last two to three years of his life. At the present we have no means of knowing whether those were written down during his lifetime or not; possibly some people took down notes of them, and possibly some followers committed them to memory. After quite some time when the Gospels were composed, these sermons and sayings of Jesus were integrated into those works. Hence, the Evangel mentioned in the Qur'an does not refer to the four Gospels, but to the sum total of the above-mentioned fragments which consist of the sermons and sayings attributed to Jesus. We also have no means of distinguishing those fragments from the exegetical comments of the composers of the Gospels; hence, at best, we may treat the statements attributed to Jesus – and those alone – as genuine parts of the Evangel. The Qur'an confirms only this portion of the Gospels, and, were one to compare the teachings embodied in these fragments, one would scarcely find any discrepancy between them and the teachings of the Qur'an (paraphrased and summarised from Mawdudi, *Tafhim al-Qur'än,* vol. I, chap. 3, n. 2, pp. 231 ff.).

That both the Jews and Christians did not take the pains needed to preserve the Scriptures in their original form, and that they even concealed their contents and wilfully distorted them, has been emphasized in the Qur'an itself. See Qur'an 2:75 and 79, 3:70-71; 3:78. This point has been continually stressed by Muslim theologians. See Ibn Hazm, *Al-Faslfi al-Milal wa al-Nihal,* 5 vols. (Cairo, 1317 A.H.), and Ibn Taymiyah, *Al-Jawäb*.

**Ansari, Zafar I. "Some reflections on Islamic bases for dialogue with Jews and Christians." Journal of Ecumenical Studies 14, no. 3 (June 1, 1977): 433-447. Footnotes on Page 438*

Bibliography

Aasi, Ghulam-Haider. "Christian-Muslim dialogue in the United States: a Muslim Perspective." *Currents in Theology and Mission* 33, no. 3, (2007): 213-222.

Aagaard, Anna Marie. "Proselytism and Privacy: Some Reflections on the Tantur Conference on Religious Freedom." *Ecumenical Review* 50, no. 4 (October 1, 1998): 464-471.

Abd-Allah, Umar F. "Do Christians and Muslims worship the same God?" *Christian Century* 121, no. 17

Abdul-Aziz Al-Musnad, Muhammad bin, *Fatawa Regarding Fasting and Zakah.* Riyadh ; Houston: Darussalam, 2002.

Abi-Mershed, Osama. "Degrees of interpretive autonomy: ijtihād and the constraints of competence and context in late medieval Tilimsan." *Islam and Christian-Muslim Relations* 13, no. 2 (April 1, 2002): 151-161.

Abu-Akel, Fahed. "The danger of Christian Zionism in the US." *Journal For Preachers* 29, no. 1 (January 1, 2005): 41-43.

Abu Zahrah, Muhammad. *The Four Imams*. 2nd ed. ed. London: Dar Al-Taqwa, 2005.

Al-Jaza'iry, Abu Bakr Jabir. *Minhaj Al-Muslim*. Riyadh: Darussalam, 2001.

Ali, Abdullah Yusuf. *An English Interpretation of the Holy Qur-an with Full Arabic Text*. Lahore: Sh. Mu-hammad Ashraf, 1976.

Ali, Mubarak. *The Muslim Handbook*. Toronto, Canada: TSP, 2001.

Alireza, Marianne. *At the Drop of a Veil / Marianne Alireza*. Costa Mesa, Calif.: Blind Owl Press, 2002.

Ameen, Abu'l-Mundhir Khaleel ibn Ibraaheem. *The Jinn and Human Sickness*. Riyadh: Houston: Darussalam, 2005.

Ansari, Zafar I. "Some reflections on Islamic bases for dialogue with Jews and Christians." *Journal of Ecumenical Studies* 14, no. 3 (June 1, 1977): 433-447.

Armstrong, Karen. *Muhammad: A Biography of the Prophet.* 1st U.S. ed. [San Francisco, Calif.]: HarperSanFrancisco, 1992.

Atiya, Nayra. *Khul-Khaal, Five Egyptian Women Tell Their Stories.* 1st ed. Contemporary Issues in the Middle East. Syracuse, N.Y.: Syracuse University Press, 1982.

Ba'Albaki, Rohi. *Al-Mawrid: A Modern English-Arabic Dictionary.* Dar El-Ilm, Lil-Malayen, Beirut Lebanon: 1993.

_________. *Al-Mawrid: A Modern Arabic-English Dictionary.* Dar El-Ilm, Lil-Malayen, Beirut Lebanon: 1988.

Ball, C., & Haque, A.. "Diversity in religious practice: Implications of Islamic values in the public workplace." *Public Personnel Management, 32* (2003) 315-330.

Barkun, Michael. "Religion and secrecy after September 11." *Journal of the American Academy of Religion* 74, no. 2 (June 1, 2006): 275-301.

Betts, Robert Brenton. *Christians in the Arab East: A Political Study.* Rev. ed. Atlanta: John Knox Press, 1978.

"Blasphemy in Pakistan." *Christian Century.* 112, no. 8 (March 8, 1995): 262-318.

Boucer, Christopher. 2008. "Saudi Arabia's "Soft" Counterterrorism Strategy: Prevention, Rehabilitation, and Aftercare" *Carnegie Endowment for International Peace.* no 97 (September 2008).

Brooks, Geraldine. *Nine Parts of Desire: The Hidden World of Islamic Women.* London: Hamish Hamilton, 1995.

Brown, John. *A Way in the Wilderness: A Bishop's Prayer Journey through the Arabian Peninsula.* Leicester: Chrisitans Aware, 2008.

Brown, Raymond Edward., Joseph A. Fitzmyer, and Roland E. Murphy. *The New Jerome Bible Commentary.* Bangalore: Theological Publications in India, 1991.

Brown, Steven P. "Leaving the spiritual sphere: religious expression in the public workplace." *Journal Of Church And State* 49, no. 4 (September 1, 2007): 665-682.

Bush, Andrew F. “The implications of Christian zionism for world mission.” *International Bulletin Of Missionary Research* 33, no. 3 (July 1, 2009): 144-150.

Bush, L Russ. “What is secularism.” *Southwestern Journal Of Theology* 26, no. 2 (March 1, 1984): 5-14.

Buttrich, George Arthur, ed. *The Interpreter's Dictionary of the Bible (volume 1-5, plus supplementary volume)*. Nashville: Abingdon Press, 1991.

Cate, Patrick O. “Islamic Values and the Gospel.” *Bibliotheca Sacra* 155, no. 619 (1998): 355-370.

Chandler, Paul Gordon. *Pilgrims of Christ on the Muslim Road: Exploring a New Path between Two Faiths*. Lanham, MD: Cowley Publications, 2007.

Chapman, Colin. *The Bible through Muslim Eyes, and a Christian Response*. Cambridge, England: Grove Books, 2008.

________. *Whose Promised Land?* New updated ed. A Lion Paperback. Oxford ; Batavia, Ill.: Lion Pub., 1992.

________. *Whose Holy City?*: Jerusalem and the Future of Peace in the Middle East. Grand Rapids, MI: Baker Books, 2005.

Cirillo, Ron. “Imagining humane realism: moving from sacred secularism toward a pragmatic theory of human rights.” *Political Theology* 11, no. 2 (March 1, 2010): 227-245.

Connell, Evan S. *Deus Lo Volt! : Chronicle of the Crusades*. Washington, D.C.: Counterpoint, 2000.

Constantelos, Demetrios J. 1978. “The “neomartyrs” as evidence for methods and motives leading to conversion and martyrdom in the Ottoman Empire.” *Greek Orthodox Theological Review* 23, no. 3-4: 216-234.

Cosmin, Barry A, and Juhem Nararro-Rivera. “The Transformation of Generation X: Shifts in Religious and Political Self-Identification, 1990-2008. A Report Based on the American Religious Identification Survey 2008.” *Program on Public Values* (2012).

Coulson, Noel J. *A History of Islamic Law* Islamic Surveys: Edinburgh: Edinburgh University Press, 1964 (1994 printing).

Cousins, Ewert. "Judaism – Christianity – Islam: Facing Modernity Together." *Journal of Ecumenical Studies* 30:3-4 (Summer-Fall 1993): 417-425.

Cox, Caroline. "How Apin Akot Redeemed His Daughter." *Christianity Today* 42, no. 3 (March 2, 1998): 56.

Cragg, Kenneth. *The Call of the Minaret.* 2nd ed. Maryknoll, N.Y.: Orbis, 1985.

________. *The Arab Christian : A History in the Middle East.* 1st ed. Louisville, Ky.: Westminster/John Knox Press, 1991.

________. *Troubled by Truth*: Biographies in the Presence of Mystery. Cleveland, Ohio: Pilgrim Press, 1994.

________. *Am I Not Your Lord? : Human Meaning in Divine Question.* London: Melisende, 2002.

Daiches, David. *Moses.* New York: Praeger Publishers, 1975.

Dalrymple, William. *From the Holy Mountain: A Journey in the Shadow of Byzantium.* London: Flamingo, 1998.

Dawood, N. J. *The Koran.* 5th rev. ed. Penguin Classics. London: Penguin, 1990.

Durán, Khalid. "Jews, Christians, Muslims – Working Together for Modernity," *Journal of Ecumenical Studies 30:3-4* (Summer-Fall 1993): 426-434.

Elmer, Duane. *Cross-Cultural Conflict : Building Relationships for Effective Ministry.* Downers Grove, Ill.: InterVarsity Press, 1993.

Ezzati, A. "Islamic law and the challenges of modern times." *Journal of Shi'a Islamic Studies* 3, no. 1 (December 1, 2010): 41-57.

Fareed, Muneer Goolam. "Against ijtihād." *Muslim World* 91, no. 3-4 (September 1, 2001): 355-370.

Fisher, Max. 2009. "Applying Saudi Counterterrorism to the Afghanistan War." *The Atlantic*. October 16, 2009.

Friedman, Daniel. "Christian Zionism and its impact on U.S. foreign policy." *Religious Studies And Theology* 28, no. 1 (January 1, 2009): 47-62.

Friedman, Thomas L. *From Beirut to Jersusalem*: Farrar, Straus and Giroux, 1989.

Fuchs-Kremer, Nancy, "Jews, Christians, and Muslims Face Modernity Together," *Journal of Ecumenical Studies* 30:3-4 (Summer-Fall 1993): 435-441

Gabrieli, Francesco. *Arab Historians of the Crusades* The Islamic World Series. London,: Routledge & Kegan Paul, 1969.

Gardner, Frank. *Blood & Sand : Love, Death and Survival in an Age of Global Terror*, Frank Gardner. (Large print ed. ed. Bath: BBC), 2006.

Glassé, Cyril. The New *Encyclopedia of Islam*. Rev. ed. Walnut Creek, CA: AltaMira Press, 2001.

Grafton, David D. "The Arab shaykh: authority in Christian and Muslim communities, and questions of social-political reform." *Islam And Christian-Muslim Relations* 23, no. 1 (January 1, 2012): 19-30.

__________. "The use of scripture in the current Israeli-Palestinian conflict." *Word & World* 24, no. 1 (2004): 29-39.

Gross, Rita M. "Religious Diversity : Some Implications for Monotheism." *Cross Currents* 49, no. 3 (September 1, 1999): 349-366.

Guth, Stephan. "Individuality lost, fun gained: some recurrent motifs in late twentieth-century Arabic and Turkish novels." *Journal of Arabic and Islamic Studies* 7, (January 1, 2007): 25-49.

Habib, John S. *Ibn Sa'ud's Warriors of Islam : The Ikhwan of Najd and Their Role in the Creation of the Sa'udi Kingdom.* 1910-1930, Leiden, The Netherlands: E. J. Brill, 1978.

Haddad, Yvonne Yazbeck. "Muslim revivalist thought in the Arab world : an overview." *Muslim World* 76, no. 3-4 (July 1, 1986): 143-167.

Halliday, Fred. "The Politics of the Umma: States and Community in Islamic Movements." *Mediterranean Politics* 7, no. 3 (November 2002): 20-41.

Halstead, J Mark. 2007. "Islamic values: a distinctive framework for moral education?" *Journal of Moral Education* 36, no.3:283.

Haney, Marsha Snulligan. "Envisioning Islam: Imam Mohammed and interfaith dialogue." *Muslim World* 99, no. 4 (October 1, 2009): 608-634.

Haq, S Nomanul. "Revisiting the question of Islam and violence." *Dialog* 40, no. 4 (December 1, 2001): 302-306.

Hassan, Riaz. "On being religious: patterns of religious commitment in Muslim societies." *Muslim World* 97, no. 3 (July 1, 2007): 437-478.

Hiebert, Paul G. "Cultural Differences and the Communication of the Gospel (Perspectives On the World Christian Movement)." *Wm Carey Library Press* (1981): 373-83.

Hille, Rolf. 2006. "Human rights and Islam -- is the 'clash of civilizations' already pre-programmed?." *Evangelical Review of Theology* 30, no. 4: 352-361.

Hillenbrand, Carole. "The Islamic world and the Crusades." *Scottish Journal Of Religious Studies* 7, no. 2 (September 1, 1986): 150-157.

Hiro, Dilip. *Dictionary of the Middle East*. New York: St. Martin's Press, 1996.

Hirschfelder, Umm AbdurRahman, and Umm Yasmeen Rahmaan. *From Monogamy to Polygyny : A Way Through*. 1st ed. Riyadh ; Houston: Darussalam, 2003.

Ho, Wai-Yip. "Danish cartoon controversy in the Chinese context: transnational Islam and public visibility of Hong Kong Muslims." *Contemporary Islam* 3, no. 3 (October 1, 2009): 275-293.

Hooker, R. H., and Christopher Lamb. *Love the Stranger: Ministry in Multi-Faith Areas* New Library of Pastoral Care. London: SPCK, 1986.

Hosseini, Khaled. *A Thousand Splendid Suns*. Large print ed. ed. Rearsby: W F Howes, 2007.

Howarth, David Armine. *The Desert King: The Life of Ibn Saud.* [New ed.] London: Quartet Books, 1980.

Ibn Abdul Wahhab, Imam Muhammad *Kitab at-Tawheed.* Riyadh: International Islamic Publishing House, 2002.

Ibn Kathir, Ism a il ibn Umar. *Stories of the Prophets: Peace Be Upon Them.* 1st ed. Riyadh, Saudi Arabia: Darussalam, 1999.

Ibrahim, I. A. *A Brief Illustrated Guide to Understanding Islam.* 2nd ed. Houston: Darussalam, 1997.

Islamic Council, 16 Grosvenor Crescent, London SW1. *Universal Islamic Declaration of Human Rights*, 1999 (accessed March 9, 2010).

Kaplan, Robert D. *Balkan Ghosts: A Journey through History.* 1st ed. New York: St. Martin's Press, 1993.

Kechichian, Joseph A. "Islamic revivalism and change in Saudi Arabia : Juhaymān al-'Utaybī's "letters" to the Saudi people." Muslim World 80, no. 1 (January 1, 1990): 1-16.

Khan, Muhammad Muhsin. *The Translation of the Meanings of Sahih Al-Bukhari, Arabic-English.* 9 vols. Riyadh, Saudi Arabia: Darussalam, 1997.

Kreinath, Jens. "Headscarf discourses and the contestation of secularism in Turkey." Council Of Societies For The Study Of Religion Bulletin 38, no. 4 (November 1, 2009): 77-84.

Layish, Aharon. "The transformation of the sharī'a from jurists' law to statutory law in the contemporary Muslim world." *Welt des Islams* 44, no. 1 (January 1, 2004): 85-113.

Lee, Clarence L. "Defense of true individuality." *Lutheran Quarterly* 17, no. 4 (November 1, 1965): 330-334.

Lewis, Bernard, "The Roots of Muslim Rage" *The Atlantic Monthly Online*; Volume 266, No. 3; September 1990, PP. 47-60.

_______. *Cultures in Conflict: Christians, Muslims, and Jews in the Age of Discovery.* New York, Oxford: Oxford University Press, 1995.

Linder, Robert D. "Christianity, politics, and secular government in the United States." *Southwestern Journal Of Theology* 26, no. 2 (March 1, 1984): 42-67.

Lings, Martin. *Muhammad: His Life Based on the Earliest Sources*. London: Islamic Texts Society : Allen & Unwin, 1983.

Little, David. 1999. "Rethinking human rights: a review essay on religion, relativism, and other matters." *Journal of Religious Ethics* 27, no. 1: 151-177.

Maalouf, Amin. *The Crusades through Arab Eyes*. London: Al Saqi, 1984.

Maalouf, Tony. *Arabs in the Shadow of Israel: The Unfolding of God's Prophetic Plan for Ishmael's Line*. Grand Rapids, MI: Kregel Publications, 2003.

Maudoodi, Syed abul Ala. *Human Rights in Islam*. Leicester: Islamic Foundation, 1976.

Mackey, Sandra. *The Saudis: Inside the Desert Kingdom*. Updated ed. New York: W.W. Norton, 2002.

Maccoby, Hyam. *The Mythmaker: Paul and the Invention of Christianity*, 1st U.S. ed. New York: Harper & Row, 1986.

Madhany, al-Husein N. "Pooh-poohing pluralism: Itjihāding Hadith to build a theology of exclusion." *Muslim World* 98, no. 4 (October 1, 2008): 407-422.

Mahfuz, Naguib. *Children of Gebelawi*. London: Heinemann, 1981.

________. *The Cairo Trilogy*. London: Black Swan, 1994.

Marr, Phebe A. "The development of a nationalist ideology in Iraq, 1920-1941." *Muslim World* 75, no. 2 (April 1, 1985): 85-101.

Maqsood, Ruqaiyyah Waris. *The Muslim Marriage Guide*. London: Quilliam, 1995.

Maudoodi, Syed Abul A'la. *Towards Understanding the Qur'an*. Liecester, UK: Islamic Foundation, 2006.

Mazrui, Ali A. Islam and the United States: streams of convergence, strands of divergence. *Third World Quarterly*, Vol. 25, No. 5, 2004: 793-820.

_______. 1997. "Islamic and Western Values." *Foreign Affairs* 76, no. 5: 118-132.

Mernissi, Fatima. *Beyond the Veil: Male-Female Dynamics in Modern Muslim Society*. Rev. ed. Bloomington: Indiana University Press, 1987.

Miller, Judith. *God Has Ninety-Nine Names: Reporting from a Militant Middle East*. New York: Simon & Schuster, 1996.

Mokhtari, Shadi. 2004. "The search for human rights within an Islamic framework in Iran." *Muslim World* 94, no. 4: 469-479.

Muslim, Imam, and Abdul Hamid Siddiqi. *Sahih Muslim Rendered into English*. Beirut: Dar al Arabia, 1972.

Novak, Michael. "Another Islam." *First Things* no. 127 (November 1, 2002): 17-18.

Nuwayhī, Muhammad. "Religion of Islam : a presentation to Christians." *International Review of Mission* 65, no. 258 (April 1, 1976): 216-225.

Osman, Ghada. "Foreign slaves in Mecca and Medina in the formative Islamic period." *Islam and Christian-Muslim Relations* 16, no. 4 (October 1, 2005): 345-359.

Ouis, Pernilla. "Islamization as a strategy for reconciliation between modernity and tradition: examples from contemporary Arab Gulf states." I*slam and Christian-Muslim Relations* 13, no. 3 (July 1, 2002): 315-334.

Owens, Virginia Stem. "The Son of Laughter." *Christianity Today* 37, no. 10 (September 13, 1993): 48-22.

Pigliucci, Massimo. 2000. "Personal gods, deism, & the limits of skepticism." *Skeptic* 8, no. 2: 38-45.

Philips, Abu Ameenah Bilaal. *The Evolution of Fiqh: Islamic Law & the Madh-Habs*. Riyadh: International Islamic Publishing House, 2000.

_______. *The Fundamentals of Tawheed.* Riyadh: International Islamic Publishing House, 2005.

Qutb, Sayyid. *Milestones*. Reprint ed. New Delhi: Islamic Book Service, 2005.

_______, John B. Hardie, and Hamid Algar. *Social Justice in Islam*. Rev. ed. Oneonta, N.Y.: Islamic Publications International, 2000.

Rabinove, Samuel. "Everybody's business--and nobody's." *Christian Century* 87, no. 27 (July 8, 1970): 843-846.

Rahner, Karl. *Encyclopedia of Theology, The Concise Sacramundum Mundi*. New York, The Seabury Press, 1975.

Rashid, Nasser Ibrahim, and Esber I. Shaheen. *Saudi Arabia : All You Need to Know*. Joplin, Mo.: International Institute of Technology, 1995.

Rashid, Tahmina. "Secular State, Citizenship and the Matrix of Globalized Religious Identity." *Alternatives: Turkish Journal of International Relations* 6, no. 1&2 (Spring & Summer 2007): 156-175.

Read, Jen'nan Ghazal. "The sources of gender role attitudes among Christian and Muslim Arab-American women." *Sociology of Religion* 64, no. 2 (June 1, 2003): 207-222.

_______. "Challenging myths of Muslim women: the influence of Islam on Arab-American women's labor force activity." *Muslim World* 92, no. 1-2 (March 1, 2002): 19-37.

Rifat, Alifah, and Denys Johnson-Davies. *Distant View of a Minaret and Other Stories*. London ; New York: Quartet Books, 1983.

Roberson, B. A. *Shaping the Current Islamic Reformation* History and Society in the Islamic World. London ; Portland, OR: Frank Cass, 2003.

Saab, Hassan. 1964. "Sacred and the profane in Islamic culture." *Journal of Religious Thought* 20, no. 2: 147.

Salibi, Kamal S. *A House of Many Mansions : The History of Lebanon Reconsidered*. Berkeley: University of California Press, 1988.

Schimmel, Annemarie. *Mystical Dimensions of Islam*. Chapel Hill: University of North Carolina Press, 1975.

Scudder, Lewis R. *The Arabian Mission's Story: In Search of Abraham's Other Son* The Historical Series of the Reformed Church in America No. 30. Grand Rapids, Mich.: Wm. B. Eerdmans Pub., 1998.

Shabi, Rachel. *We Look Like the Enemy : The Hidden Story of Israel's Jews from Arab Lands.* 1st U.S. ed. New York: Walker & Co., 2008.

Shad, Abdur Rehman. *Muslim Etiquettes*. 2nd ed. Lahore: Kazi Publications, 1985.

Shah, Idries. *Tales of the Dervishes*: New York, Dutton, 1969 [c1967], 1993.

Shalhub, Fuad ibn Abd al-Az iz. *The Book of Manners*. 1st ed. Riyadh ; Houston: Darussalam, 2003.

Sieny, Muhammed Esma'il. *Heroes of Islam.* Riyadh: International Islamic Publishing House, 2000.

Skinner, Ray F. *Christians in Oman*. Modern: Tower Press, 1995.

Smith, Huston. *The Religions of Man.* 1st Perennial Library ed. New York: Perennial Library, 1989.

Smith, Jane I. "Women in Islam: Equity, equality, and the search for the natural order." J*ournal of the American Academy of Religion* 47, no. 4 (December 1, 1979): 517-537.

Sonnack, Paul G. "Church and state in light of the doctrine of the two kingdoms." *Word & World* 4, no. 3 (June 1, 1984): 269-277.

Souaiaia, Ahmed E. "Reasoned and inspired beliefs: a study of Islamic theology." *Muslim World* 97, no. 2 (April 1, 2007): 331-349.

Stegner, Wallace Earle. *Discovery; the Search for Arabian Oil* An Export Book. Beirut, Lebanon,: Printed by Middle East Export Press, 1971.

Tahmina, Rashid. "Secular State, Citizenship and the Matrix of Globalized Religious Identity." *Turkish Journal of International Relations*, Vo. 6, No. 1 & 2, Spring & Summer, 2007: 156-175.

Tamimi, Azzam, and John L. Esposito. *Islam and Secularism in the Middle East.* London: Hurst & Company, 2000.

Taylor, Julie Anne. "Freedom and bondage among Muslims in southern Italy during the thirteenth century." *Journal of Muslim Minority Affairs* 27, no. 1 (April 1, 2007): 71-77.

Thesiger, Wilfred. *The Marsh Arabs*. London: Longmans, 1964.

Toffolo, Cris E., and Charles Amjad-Ali. "Christians in Pakistan confront charges of blasphemy." *Christian Century* 115, no. 21 (July 29, 1998): 716-718.

von Denffer, Ahmed. *Christians in the Qur'an and the Sunna*. Leicester, UK: The Islamic Foundation, 1987.

Von Sicard, Sigvard. 1976. "Contemporary Islam and its world mission." *Missiology* 4, no. 3: 343-361.

Volf, Miroslav. *Allah: A Christian Response.* New York: Harper Collins, 2011.

Watt, W. Montgomery. *Muhammad: Prophet and Statesman* A Galaxy Book,. London, New York: Oxford University Press, 1974.

_______. "Islamic attitudes to cultural borrowing." *Scottish Journal Of Religious Studies* 7, no. 2 (September 1, 1986): 141-149.

Weeramantry, C.G. *Islamic Jurisprudence, An International Perspective.* Ratmalana, Sri Lanka: Vishva Lehkh Publishers, 1998.

Wehr, Hans, and J. Milton Cowan. *A Dictionary of Modern Written Arabic (Arab.-Engl.)*. 4. ed. Wiesbaden: Harrassowitz, 1979.

White, Andrew. *The Vicar of Baghdad: Fighting for Peace in the Middle East.* Oxford, UK: Monarch Books, 2009.

Woodberry, J Dudley. "The Muslim Understanding of Jesus." *Word & World* 16, no. 2 (March 1, 1996): 173-178.

Yancey, Philip. "How we became the "Great Satan." *Christianity Today* 35, no. 5 (April 29, 1991): 64.

Zahl, Paul F. M., and Paul Basden. *Exploring the Worship Spectrum : 6 Views* Counterpoints. Grand Rapids, Mich.: Zondervan, 2004.

Zeno, Muhammad bin Jamil. *The Pillars of Islam and Iman*. Riyadh, Saudi Arabia: Darussalam Publications, 1996.

Zia Ullah, Muhammad. *Islamic Concept of God*. London; Boston: Kegan Paul International, 1984.

Zuhur, Sherifa. *Revealing Reveiling: Islamist Gender Ideology in Contemporary Egypt*. State University of New York Press, 1 Jul 1992.

Zwemer, Samuel Marinus. "The Allah of Islam and the God of Jesus Christ." *Theology Today* 3, no. 1 (April 1, 1946): 64-77.